"I believe the time to change is now. *Ignite!* sets leaders on course to make a significant difference in themselves, their people, and their teams."
Marshall Goldsmith, million-selling author of *New York Times* best sellers *MOJO* and *What Got You Here Won't Get You There*

"I found *Ignite!* to be one of the best leadership books I've read. Sal does an excellent job of mixing in work and leisure activities as a way to make his points around putting people first—it was an easy but powerful read!"
Von Rhea, Director, Software Development, GHX

"*Ignite!* has had a significant impact in helping our emerging leaders transition from individual contributors to managers, and in helping our senior leaders effectively coach them."
Jill Scott, Director of Human Resources, Professional Finance Company

"Whether you are a veteran leader or a first-time leader, this book will help you rethink the way you lead in every aspect of your life."
Matthew Kelly, *New York Times* bestselling author of *The Dream Manager* and *Off Balance*

"Having read several business books over the past twenty-five years, I find Sal's book *Ignite!* to be THE most practical guide to managing and leading a team. Sal clearly describes the methods for establishing yourself as a leader, then shaping a team culture to achieve high-performance results for an organization. Sal also provides examples of typical pitfalls that can limit the manager's and team's potential. This book is thorough, well-written, and should inspire any manager to become a better leader."
Randy Briggs, Senior Sourcing Manager, Vaisala, Inc.

"*Ignite!* is a must-read for any leader at any level of an organization. Sal Silvester's insightful yet practical leadership processes will help make any leader and his or her people a great success. As the book so clearly demonstrates, leadership effectiveness is about putting 'people first.' Most of us don't naturally do that—another reason this book is a must-read."

Al Ritter, President, Ritter Consulting Group, and author of *Life is a Paradox* and *The 100/0 Principle*

Ignite!

The 4 Essential Rules for Emerging Leaders

By Sal Silvester
303-579-5829
sal@512solutions.com
http://www.512solutions.com

20660 Stevens Creek Blvd., Suite 210
Cupertino, CA 95014

Contents

Igniting the Potential of Emerging Leaders

Here is what I know about you: I'll bet you are smart and successful, maybe even a rising star in your organization. You're considered the go-to person on your team. You're so good at your job—as an engineer, financial analyst, customer-service representative, software developer, nurse, sales representative—that people are taking notice, and something is about to rock your world.

You are about to get promoted.

The problem is, if you are like many other new or recently promoted managers, you feel thoroughly unprepared and out of your element. Perhaps even a bit scared.

And with good reason. Like so many who have greatness thrust upon them, this is all new and unfamiliar to you. How you handle the often-rocky transition to managing people will affect not only your future, but also that of your company. As a front-line leader, your actions have a direct impact on your team members' level of engagement, productivity, job satisfaction, morale, and commitment, more so than any other factor in your organization.

According to the Gartner Group, people don't leave their organizations. They leave their managers. Suddenly...that's *you*.

Just thinking about what's at stake can be over-whelming—especially since in most organiza-tions, new managers don't receive a bit of leadership training before being dispatched to the front lines.

We often hear that leadership is about charis-matic people who inspire others through the force of their personality. Or that leadership is an innate set of characteristics magically bestowed upon the lucky ones at birth. Or that you have to join the Army and complete Special Forces training as a rite of passage into the discipline and godliness of leadership.

None of that is true. The essence of leadership is about employing key skills and behaviors on a consistent basis. The good news? These skills and behaviors can be learned. *Seriously.*

That's right, leadership can be learned. And guess what? *It's not too late.* You can learn these skills and become an effective and influential leader, starting today.

This book provides rising stars like you with a practical model that can be implemented imme-diately to help ignite your leadership potential. You'll learn the four essential rules to live by that will enable you to generate commitment from your team members.

This book is not just for emerging leaders. It's also for senior leaders to whom the emerging ones report, and who play a key role in develop-ing the next generation of leaders. In the best or-ganizations, they're busy coaching, teaching, and imparting the experiences that help promising candidates to develop and eventually take on more senior roles. That not only helps the organization deepen its bench strength, it enables senior leaders to focus on more strategic roles as they relinquish some of the day-to-day challenges of running the business.

Good leadership isn't something you can memorize, like the multiplication tables. How then can you learn about and embody this allegedly mythical, magical set of qualities?

The best teaching tool I know of is the learning parable. It's a story about a fictional person with real-life business and leadership challenges that illustrates all the essential elements of what you're trying to learn. In the first part of this book, you'll meet Ben Turner, the main character in our learning parable. Ben is a technology expert in the Professional Services Department at BCO-Tek, a $150 million software development company with more than one hundred employees based in Boulder, Colorado. Ben likes his job fine just the way it is, and greets the unexpected news of his promotion as he would a sudden case of the flu. But now, if Ben can't figure out how to get his team members moving in the same direction, not only will his career prospects diminish, his company will lose critical customers to the competition.

Although Ben is a fictional character, stories like his are playing out within large and small companies across the nation in increasing numbers—with potentially devastating effects on the bottom line as companies put their trust in newly emerging leaders who aren't quite ready for prime time. Ben's story illustrates the pitfalls and possibilities of leadership at every turn, but it is more than just a story. It incorporates for the first time the **People-First Leadership™** model as developed from my twenty-plus years of experience as an Army officer and an executive at Accenture, and in the field on hundreds of client engagements as a management consultant at my company, 5.12 Solutions.

In the second section of this book, I outline a powerful and actionable four-point leadership model that will give you all the tools you need to elevate your effectiveness and gain the commitment of your people. I'll take you step by step through the four-part **People-First Leadership Model** illustrated by Ben's story so that you can understand and implement the key skills and behaviors required of *all* leaders, whether emerging or senior. This is the same model I use with my clients in person, and I want to share it with you.

People first.

Sal Silvester
January 2012
Boulder, Colorado

I Ben's Climb: A Leadership Story

1 The Same Old

At 9:07 a.m., the last person finally strolled into the conference room, but at BCO-Tek, this was normal. People counted on meetings never starting on time. The key was to arrive late enough not to have to wait too long for the others, but not so late as to be the last one in.

Ben Turner was the acknowledged master of the game of late-but-not-too-late. He had arrived at precisely four minutes past the hour. Despite his five-foot-nine stature, his technical knowledge and fast pace were intimidating. He loved to rock climb on weekends and hit the gym weekdays, but at work he was all business. As a result, Ben had developed a reputation as the go-to technical guy, and it wasn't uncommon for Stephanie, the VP of Professional Services, to solicit his advice. Even members of the executive team often consulted him.

BCO-Tek started out as a two-person software development shop in the garage of one of the founders. After struggling over what to call the company, they named it after their hometown of Boulder, Colorado. At first, they took on small web-based projects for local banks, but over time, they developed a product that helped financial institutions consolidate investment data for their customers. In just ten years BCO-Tek had grown to over $150 million in annual revenues and more than 150 employees. Its modern downtown office had sweeping views of the foothills to the west of Boulder, and its open design gave off a vibe of simple sophistication.

Professional Services was responsible for customizing and implementing client solutions. Along with Ben, his department consisted of Angela, Jen, Kevin, and John. Ben had been with BCO-Tek almost since its inception, and had several unspoken privileges that came with being the No. 9 person in the company; just having a rank within the Top 10 was its own status symbol.

Angela was the newest, youngest, and greenest member of the team. She had already been in the room since three minutes to nine when Ben waltzed in, which was how you could tell she was new. She had come straight from the Leeds School of Business at the University of Colorado, and the standard "on-boarding" process had done little to prepare her for the real culture at BCO-Tek—including being late-but-not-too-late—but she could barely contain her excitement over starting her first "real" job, and interacting with so many smart and interesting people. The possibilities for her at BCO-Tek seemed endless.

"Hey, Angela," said Ben. "What's the status on the conversion error issue?"

She had hopped up from her chair to bounce over to greet him, but halted mid-bounce at his right-down-to-business tone, and froze in confusion. "Oh, right, " she said, her eyes darting away. "I didn't realize it was due this early. Heh, guess I should have had more coffee!" She shot back to her seat and quickly scribbled a Note to Self. She was relieved to see Kevin and Jen arrive.

Kevin was lanky with a light complexion and reddish-blond hair, and as a senior consultant was only a few years junior to Ben. He had been with the company almost four years and could figure out just about anything, from product code and back-end database to networking issues. He placed his iPad directly in front of him, taking an extra three seconds to make sure it was perfectly aligned with the edge of the conference table.

Chapter 1: The Same Old

Jen had joined BCO-Tek two years earlier after finishing her graduate work in English literature. It was unusual that someone with an arts degree would end up in a technical role, but she was a natural, a stable team member who could always be counted on. She was reserved but consistent, and happiest when she could work with others to accomplish a task.

At seven minutes past the hour, the team manager walked in. John had been with BCO-Tek only ten months, after several years with one of the big consulting firms. He certainly knew how to run a project, yet relied heavily on Ben for a lot of the technical aspects. He always opened his meetings with a dose of small talk, followed by a quick informational update on whatever project was in play, but today was different. No small talk, no chitchat. "I have an announcement to make," he said, and Ben shifted uneasily in his chair.

"Folks, I'm leaving BCO-Tek," said John. "I'm giving my two weeks' notice as of today."

There was a brief, stunned silence.

"Whoa, whoa, whoa," said Ben. "Are you just gonna slip out the back, Jack, make a new plan, Stan, without filling us in?"

The outburst was not unusual for Ben. He had never been shy about challenging almost anyone in the organization, especially in situations where he felt control slipping away.

"It's been great working with you guys, but this is a big opportunity for me," John began, but Ben interrupted.

"What about the Q-Bank project?" he said. "We're right in the middle of it." Q-Bank was a recently acquired client that had switched over to BCO-Tek's platform from a competitor's, and it was critical that the implementation go smoothly. Ben didn't doubt that John had his reasons for leaving, but it would mean that Ben's already heavy workload was about to get a lot worse. How would he meet the deadlines with a new team leader first getting acclimated?

"Nothing to worry about," said John. "I've already created a transition plan and gone over it with Stephanie."

Ben didn't find that as reassuring as John probably meant it to be.

"When Stephanie's back from her management offsite, she'll follow up with everyone," John continued. "Meanwhile, well, I just wanted to deliver the news personally."

Jen was the first to recover. "Congratulations, you!" she said.

"All the best in your new gig," echoed Kevin.

"Yeah, ditto," said Ben. "But seriously, about Q-Bank..."

"Relax," said John. "All in good time."

Ben was not relaxed. He was feeling a little ill. He did a quick deep-breathing exercise, but it didn't seem to help. Then he told himself they'd probably pull in someone from Engineering to act as team leader in the interim.

Anyway, he thought, *I'm sure Stephanie has it covered.*

2 The New Deal

"Have a seat, gentlemen," said Stephanie, pointing to a small, glass-topped table in the corner of her office. "Ben, I believe you know Darryl Remington?"

The two men nodded at each other, although neither could say why the vice president had called them in for this private meeting. Darryl was a senior consultant on another project team with the Professional Services Department. Even though at six-foot-one and 165 pounds Darryl peered down on most people, he had a clumsy, nonintimidating demeanor. He was attentive and kind, more moderate in pace than Ben, and enjoyed friendly conversation.

Stephanie was neatly dressed in her usual uniform: casual slacks and a pressed blouse. At forty-one, she was able to bridge the gap between her younger generation of team members and the more senior executive banking clients.

"How's it going?" she asked them.

"Up to my ears in implementation issues," Ben replied. "Other than that, I'm good."

"Glad to hear you're good," said Stephanie with a smile. "How about you, Darryl?"

"Uh, fine," he said. "How was the management team offsite?"

"Very productive," she said. "I'm looking forward to sharing the strategic plan with your teams."

"Our what?" Ben said in alarm. *Damn, I knew this was coming.*

"I know you're both very busy, so I'll get right to the point," said Stephanie. "John's announcement took us all by surprise. Frankly, I'm disappointed he didn't give us a heads-up sooner."

"Took me by surprise, too," muttered Ben.

"You guys have both been top performers," she continued. "Ben, you're the go-to guy on the development team. Darryl, you've done a great job with the test group."

Ben tensed, waiting for the other shoe to drop. Which it promptly did.

"Congratulations," said Stephanie, breaking into a smile. "I'm promoting both of you to team leader."

Son of a...dog, dog, dog, thought Ben.

"Er, I don't understand," said Darryl. "Are we going to co-manage the team?"

"Nope," said Stephanie. "I'm dividing the team into two smaller ones—a development team led by Ben, and a testing team led by Darryl." She looked at each of them in turn. "Organizationally it makes sense, and it's something I've wanted to try ever since I took over this role."

Ben didn't realize he had sighed out loud until Stephanie asked what was on his mind.

"Why don't you just bring in a lead from Engineering?" he blurted out. "I love the technical work. I'm good at it. Clients *like* me. Managing people is the last thing I have time for right now."

Darryl opened his mouth as if to chime in, but closed it again and pressed his lips together so tightly they began to turn white.

"Guys, guys," said Stephanie, holding up a hand. "Leadership isn't about what it says on your business card. Just because you have the title of leader doesn't make you one, and just because you *don't* have that title doesn't mean you *aren't* one. People at every level of this organization have looked to both of you over the past several years for just about everything. Ben, last week you briefed the CEO on some of the challenges we're having with Q-Bank. I think it's time we made it official."

"Yeah," said Ben, "but what about...?"

"Q-Bank?" Stephanie filled in for him. "We'll shift Angela and Jen over from their other projects to work with you on it. You'll also have Kevin fifty percent of the time. And I'm thinking of hiring a new testing analyst in a few months."

She turned to Darryl, who was busily rubbing one of his eyes. "Damn allergies," he muttered.

"Darryl, you'll take the remaining folks who are already in testing roles. That will give you the people you need for completing Q-Bank on time, and for gearing up for AccuSave."

"AccuSave?" said Darryl. "You mean there's another project in the pipeline?"

"Yup. Sales just landed an enterprise implementation. Isn't that terrific? I just found out at the offsite yesterday." She beamed at them, and they both managed something resembling a smile in return. Stephanie started scrolling through the calendar program on her iPhone with her forefinger. "Let's see, you'll coordinate the kickoff meeting next Tuesday. Along with the overall project, of course."

"Of course," Darryl said in a hoarse whisper.

"Don't worry," she said. "You'll enjoy it."

"Enjoy it, yes, absolutely," said Darryl. "It's just...these allergies." He pointed apologetically in the vicinity of his throat.

I can't wait to see what sales came up with this time, Ben thought. *They always promise the world. You'd think they'd consult us before committing to an entire new implementation plan.*

"OK, here's my suggestion," said Stephanie in a getting-back-to-business voice. "Let's plan for the three of us to meet on a weekly basis so I can help you transition into your new roles." She scrolled through her phone calendar again. "Monday mornings work for you? How about right after the status meetings with your teams?"

"Sure," said Ben. Inwardly, he thought, *Whatever.*

"Awesome," said Darryl, sounding miserable.

"You guys'll set the agenda for these sessions," said Stephanie. "Come prepared."

On the way out, Ben said to Darryl under his breath, "Something tells me life as we know it is over."

"Ya think?" said Darryl.

3 First Test

Ben and Darryl had been meeting frequently with Stephanie for two weeks to help with the transition, when something new went wrong. It was the combination of an onslaught of bugs in the software, and Q-Bank making an unexpected change in the production environment that blindsided the engineers. Now they needed a new patch, and it would probably throw the project off schedule—not an acceptable option to Q-Bank. *This high-profile engagement just got higher in profile,* Ben thought with dismay.

On a Friday morning after a long week of development and testing, Ben took Darryl aside. "You know what I'm thinking?" he said.

Darryl shook his head mutely.

"There's no way we can handle this unless everyone works over the weekend."

"I was hoping you wouldn't say that," said Darryl. They both knew they were staring down the barrel of their first difficult decision as new managers. "OK then, you go tell your team, and I'll tell mine."

"If they eat me alive," said Ben, "I just want to say what a pleasure it's been knowing you." He meant to deliver the bad news right away, and he couldn't believe it when he glanced at his watch and saw it was already 2:30 p.m. *Time flies when I'm having fun...not.* When he finally caught a moment between client calls, chat messages, and talking with the engineers who needed his expertise, he called an impromptu meeting with Kevin, Angela, and Jen.

"No doubt about it, we've all gotta work this weekend," he told them, diving right in as usual. "Q-Bank won't budge on the original timeline, and Stephanie said there's no wiggle room. So, cancel your plans for tomorrow, and everyone be here in the morning at nine."

The room went silent. Shoulders slumped. Angela was about to say something, but didn't. At last, Kevin piped up. "How long do you think we'll need to be here?" he asked.

"Not sure," Ben replied. "Probably until the test team confirms we're rid of the P1s," the software bugs with the highest priority in the eyes of the client. P1s were usually the showstoppers that kept a system from going live.

"That could take hours," Kevin said.

"It is what it is," said Ben. "Any questions? No? OK, team, let's make it happen!"

"I had plans to be with my family," Angela muttered as they all trudged back to their cubicles.

"I hear ya," said Kevin. "Personally, I don't mind putting in the extra time, but at least John always used to give us a decent amount of notice."

That went pretty well, Ben mused. Even if no one was happy about it, at least they'd all know that he was also screwed, maybe more than they were. Just that day, he had been in the office since 7:00 a.m., since he liked getting some work done when there were fewer interruptions, and he often put in a couple of hours from home each night after going to the gym. He had been making sure that weekends were roped off for his newfound passions: rock climbing, mountaineering, and ice climbing, but it looked like that wasn't going to be in the cards this time. His team would feel better, knowing that Ben too was making sacrifices.

Over in the testing room, things were playing out a little differently. This was exactly what Darryl had feared about being a manager—having to impose on his people and be the bad guy. *It was so much easier when all I had to do was my job,* he thought, looking back with nostalgia to only a few weeks ago. The good old days, when he was simply responsible for testing.

First, to steel himself for what he had to do, and for the possibility that he would be voted Mr. Unpopularity, Darryl watered his office plants. Then he casually walked over to the grouping of cubicles where his team sat. "Um, excuse me?" he said. "I don't mean to interrupt you, but ..."

"What's up?" said a team member, using what Darryl thought was an unnecessarily brisk tone.

"Well, with the changes that Q-Bank made, I'm not sure we'll get it all finished by Monday."

Heads in the cubicles popped up like prairie dogs. "You're not *sure*?" asked one of them.

"I'm just saying it's a lot of work," said Darryl. "I'm kinda thinking it'd be great to spend some time over the weekend, you know?" He realized too late that the word "great" was perhaps not the best way of describing "giving up your well-earned free time."

"Like, maybe knockin' out some of the work," he continued, trying to cover his gaffe. He went into a batter's stance and swung at an imaginary ball, but he almost knocked a bud vase off of a nearby desk. "The thing is, the development team is working this weekend, and you're all invited."

"Wow, sounds like a party," he heard someone say as he hastened back to his office.

A few hours later, things weren't so happy over at Happy Hour at the West End Bar and Grill. Up on the rooftop deck of this downtown Boulder bar, Kevin, Angela, and Jen peered glumly into steins of the local microbrew draft beer. "OK, it's been real," said Jen. "I'd love to complain some more about Ben, 'cause I was just getting started, but unfortunately, I've got to get up early to be at the office."

"Gives new meaning to TGIF," Ken grumbled.

On Saturday morning, as 9:30 a.m. came and went, Kevin, Jen, and Angela began to wonder what happened to Ben. Had he overslept? Been in an accident? He hadn't even called to let them know he wouldn't be joining them in detention. "Do you think we ought to call the area hospitals and check?" Angela asked.

Around 10:30, the testing team straggled in one by one, each member noticing that the development team was already hard at work. Since Darryl had never specified a time at which they were expected to join this "party," they had made their own assumptions. Darryl was there too, but he stayed in his office with his well-watered plants and his door closed so his team wouldn't feel as if he was trying to micromanage or keep anyone under surveillance. He congratulated himself on his sensitivity to their needs.

Both teams plugged away. Conversation was sparse, and tended toward the fun they were missing, the tickets they'd given up, the friends and family they wouldn't be seeing. The development team stayed until early afternoon and decided that a few more hours on Sunday morning would do the trick. The testing team soon came to the same conclusion.

Everyone was back in the office by 9:00 a.m. the next day—except for Ben, who was still MIA. And then they heard it: the unmistakable sound of the security code being punched into the office suite door. It was Ben, not fresh from some hospital emergency room, but looking quite healthy in sneakers, shorts, a Lycra jersey, and a sun visor.

"Enjoy your run?" asked Jen drily.

"Yeah, thanks," said Ben. "How are those bug fixes coming along, people?"

"Working through it," said Kevin. "By the way, where've you been?"

Before Ben could reply, Angela let out an unexpected "ughhh" of frustration. "I thought Engineering fixed this issue!" she said with dismay. Kevin went over to help her, so Ben was satisfied that everything was being attended to. He sauntered over to his cube, checked his e-mail, fired off a few IMs, and after about thirty minutes walked out of the office without so much as a goodbye. He knew his team would understand how much he gave up—that he'd be back at his home office, burning the midnight oil well after the others were already out at their picnics and having fun. Ben would just have to live with the sacrifices he made.

4 Stephanie's Whiteboard

Ben and Darryl were pretty psyched. Working the weekend hadn't been fun, but they had managed to tackle their first real challenge as leaders and get the new patch over to Q-Bank in time for the Monday morning status call. They high-fived each other as they made their way to Stephanie's office for the weekly coaching session.

"Tell me," she said when the three of them were again seated at the round, glass-topped table. "Why do you think this weekend was a bust?"

"Excuse me?" Ben practically roared. "Ask anyone, it went spectacularly well."

"How so?"

Ben described the events of the weekend defensively, ending with, "They all know I work my butt off. I'm in earlier; I work later. I gave up my entire weekend by working from home."

"I know how hard you work," Stephanie said in a quiet, neutral voice that made Ben realize how strident he must have sounded. "But people value different things, and your credibility as a leader goes well beyond simply working your butt off."

"What do you mean?"

"Leadership begins with credibility and trust," said Stephanie. "Think about it. Have you ever respected a manager you felt wasn't credible and trustworthy?"

It took Ben a while to come up with an answer. He was half-hoping that Stephanie would fill in the silence herself, but she waited patiently, as she always did.

"I guess not," Ben said finally. "In my last job, I worked for a guy I couldn't stand."

"What exactly couldn't you stand about him?"

"He didn't have the technical skills to be a team leader. He was hands-off, barely around, never seemed to know what he was doing."

"I see," said Stephanie. "It sounds like to you, credibility is about competence and being able to walk the talk. So tell me, did you trust this man?"

"No way," said Ben. "He was nice and all, but I always worried when he was off in a meeting with upper management that he was signing us up for things where he didn't understand the ramifications. We never knew what was coming."

"How about you, Darryl?" Stephanie asked. "And how are those allergies doing?"

Darryl quickly straightened his spine and made eye contact, then slumped and coughed, thumping his chest with a fist. "Uh, I was in the office all weekend," he mumbled.

"Yes, but I was asking about any managers you've had where you respected them but didn't trust them," she prodded.

"Oh, right," said Darryl. "Sorry. Well, this one guy was always changing the plan. He was totally random with what direction he took on any given day, so we never had any idea which end was up."

"So for you, Darryl, it sounds like credibility is partly about having clear performance expectations," Stephanie echoed. "Did you trust this guy?"

"Oh no, not at all," said Darryl. "It got to a point where when he'd assign a task and I couldn't be sure we weren't going to end up having to redo it anyway. I didn't trust that he valued my work."

"Good," said Stephanie. "Now relate this back to your own positions as new leaders, both of you. You have to establish credibility and trust with your people."

"I just want you to know that I am extremely in favor of credibility and trust," said Ben. "But, uh, where do we start?"

"You both just told me about leaders who didn't do a good job establishing credibility with you," said Stephanie. "Now tell me about the leader in your life you've admired most."

"Oh, that's easy," said Ben. He was always telling anyone who would listen about his new climbing habit. "I really liked Roy, the guide I had last summer when I did Longs Peak in Rocky Mountain National Park. I totally trusted him, and we were at 14,000 feet above sea level."

"Yes, but *why* did you trust him? What did he do that gave you a positive feeling?"

"He knew his stuff. He was a great climber, and strong. He wasn't shy about doing the hard work. He double-checked our gear. He looked out for us on the mountain. It was as if he put his own needs last."

"Guys," said Stephanie, "the traits Ben just described are what I call Leading by Example. This is the foundation of leadership. It's the answer to how you begin to establish credibility and trust. As leaders, we—I'm including myself here—have to model the behaviors we want to see in our people."

She glanced at her watch. "I've got a client meeting, so let's continue this conversation tomorrow. In the meantime, I've just thought of a little assignment. Has either of you ever seen the film *We Were Soldiers*? No? If you're not busy tonight, it's playing downtown."

"You want us to go to the movies?" said Darryl. "Really?" But Ben wasn't surprised by the assignment. Stephanie had started her career with four years of active duty as an Army officer, and had even been through airborne school.

That night, Ben and Darryl went to the movies. *We Were Soldiers* was playing at a local revival theater, a former opera house built in 1906. The film was intense and sometimes hard to watch, but they exited the theater in a state of euphoria.

"Man, that was powerful," said Ben.

"Yeah," said Darryl. "I keep coming back to the part where the lieutenant colonel says, 'I will be the first on the field of battle and the last to leave.'"

When they reported their reactions to Stephanie the next day, she got up and went over to her most cherished piece of office equipment: her whiteboard. She was always using it in meetings. Ben liked to joke that she probably had another one at home where normal people would have a treasured family heirloom. Stephanie picked out a purple highlighter and drew a large circle. Inside, she drew a smaller one. Inside the smaller one she wrote People, and over the top outer rim of the larger circle she wrote Lead by Example.

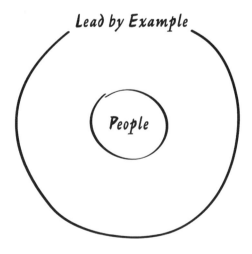

Ben and Darryl weren't entirely sure what they were looking at, but they nodded.

"If there's one thing I've learned," said Stephanie, "it's that leadership is all about people. To lead effectively, our people have to come first. I call it People-First leadership."

Darryl nodded. "People," he repeated respectfully.

"To be an effective leader, you have to start with yourself," said Stephanie. "Here, I'll be more specific: Like I said the other day, your actions and your words must be aligned. You have to, as they say, walk the talk. Leading by example is the most important component of building credibility and trust."

Stephanie smiled benignly at the whiteboard. "In the Army we used to call this 'lead the way.' We lived by a mantra of never asking a soldier to do something we wouldn't do first. It's the same in business. If you want your people to respect you, they have to believe you're credible, and that means leading by example."

"Take a bullet for them, huh?" Ben joked nervously.

"Those people who work for you," said Stephanie, "they're paying attention to what you do *and* what you don't do. They don't miss a thing."

"Don't miss a thing," repeated Darryl, falling into despondence.

"Given that," Stephanie continued, "is there anything you'd have done differently last weekend?"

Ben, as usual, went first. "I guess I should've been in the office Saturday morning—even though I worked late Friday while everyone was out at Happy Hour. And," he added, "I probably put in more hours at home on Saturday than anyone."

"How about you, Darryl?" Stephanie asked.

"Well, uh," he said. "I don't mean to throw Ben under the proverbial bus, but I was the first one here this weekend and the last to leave. And I purposely didn't bother anyone so they'd be able to get their work done as quickly as possible."

"Well, that's a start," said Stephanie. "But leading by example also means being aware of what you are *not* doing—because your team members notice that, too."

"I think I know what you're hinting at," said Darryl with a sigh. "I guess I have a tendency to sorta not be so direct. I kinda hate being the bearer of bad news."

"I'm glad you recognize that, Darryl," said Stephanie, "because part of your job as a leader, and part of leading by example, means communicating your expectations assertively and in a way that is clear to your people."

"That's not an issue for me," said Ben, and everyone chuckled.

Stephanie looked back at Darryl and said, "And an overly indirect style is not only confusing, it's disruptive and creates resentment. Remember, your people pay attention not only to your actions, but to your inaction." She crossed her legs and put one hand on top of the other as they rested on her thighs, then shifted her focus to take in both men. "Your team members need to know you're their leader both from your communication and your actions. People want to see their leader leading, just like Lieutenant Colonel Moore in the movie you saw last night. His intent was communicated clearly, and he followed through with his actions. He was first on the field of battle and last to leave. Can you imagine the trust that must have inspired?"

She asked Ben what he thought he might do differently when he left her office that day. He had to pause for a moment to reflect. "I'll follow through in a way that's more visible to my people."

"And you, Darryl?"

"Um, I guess I was pretty unclear about what I expected from my team," Darryl responded. "As much as I hate being the bad guy, I suppose I'll have to try to be, like, more assertive."

"Don't *try* to be more assertive," said Stephanie. "Don't *guess* you will. Just *be* more assertive."

"Okeydokey," said Darryl.

"Wonderful," said Stephanie, leaning back and signaling that the tough part was over. "Climbing this weekend, Ben?" she asked conversationally. She too loved to climb, and it was a topic over which they had originally bonded when Stephanie first arrived at BCO-Tek.

"Yes, ma'am," Ben replied. "Headin' to Eldo," the affectionate name climbers had for Eldorado Canyon State Park in South Boulder. It had some of the most amazing sandstone cliffs in the country, and attracted climbers from all over the world.

"And you, Darryl? What are you up to?"

"My wife's family is in town."

"Great," said Stephanie. "Well, have fun guys. And thanks for getting that patch out to Q-Bank. You went above and beyond to make it happen. Let me know if you need anything this week."

In the hall outside Stephanie's office, Ben said, "If everyone would just do their job, we wouldn't have to baby them all the time."

5 Beginning the Ascent

Early Saturday morning, Ben fumbled around the garage, threw his rope and climbing gear into the back of his black cab-covered Toyota Tacoma, grabbed a quick cup of coffee, and headed out. When William had said, "Let's get there early," he wasn't kidding. Eldorado Canyon was a popular place to climb, and with all the press it kept getting, the "classic" routes were becoming jammed with traffic. William wanted to be hiking by 6:00 a.m., which meant a five o'clock wake-up.

William was a local climbing legend who had put up several first ascents in Boulder and Eldorado canyons. Now in his early fifties, he was still climbing stronger than most twenty-year-olds. Ben had met him a few years ago during a competition at one of the local climbing gyms, when Ben was just starting out, and William had taken notice and offered advice during the "comp." They became fast friends, although Ben couldn't figure out at first why someone like William would take any interest in a newbie when he could go climbing with almost anyone. "I've had a lot of mentors in my life—both in the climbing world and at work," William had explained. "This is my opportunity to give back." And that was that. Ever since then, they went for a climb together every three or four weeks.

Ben arrived at the trailhead eight minutes late. He was so accustomed to those late meeting starts at BCO-Tek that it didn't seem like a big deal, so he was surprised when William seemed a bit put out. "Hurry up," said William by way of greeting. "My gear's already organized, so we'll take my rack and your rope."

"Good morning to you too, sunshine," said Ben, but William ignored him, hoisting his pack and starting up the dirt road, waiting at the trail junction for Ben to catch up.

The approach to the base of their route involved a twenty-minute hike up a steep trail along the base of the rock, a small patch of Class 3 scrambling, and then climbing a ladder to bridge sections of the trail. Today they were taking a route known as Yellow Spur—a six-pitch, 500-foot-plus route that wandered up the Redgarden Wall towering over South Boulder Creek. In the spring, "creek" was a misnomer. The river was so loud and powerful from the snowpack runoff that it was often difficult to hear each other, even several hundred feet up. And it was so narrow, rocky, and steep that most kayakers, the sane ones, wouldn't attempt it.

William was the first to arrive at Yellow Spur, and there was a two-person climbing team just ahead of them. Unfortunately, that meant William and Ben would be climbing underneath the other team the whole time. Not something to look forward to, as Eldo was known for its loose rock. "That's why we show up on time," said William, but he decided to go anyway, after first waiting half an hour to give the others some room.

William volunteered to take the first pitch. Even though it had a moderate rating of 5.9+, it had a funky first move to clip an already existing piton, then a thirty-foot slippery traverse to the left, followed by a short overhang that required a heel hook and another clip to an old piton. They moved pretty efficiently through the first three pitches—so much so that they caught up to the early bird climbers at the beginning of the fourth pitch, and had to clip into their anchor and sit and wait on the large Red Ledge until it was safe to continue. Ben was glad that William didn't continue to give him a hard time about those eight late minutes that would have made all the difference in their day.

They chatted about this and that, and when William asked about work, Ben told him of his promotion to development team leader.

"That's awesome," said William.

"Nah, it's a headache," said Ben. "Now I have to do my job *and* babysit three other people. My boss already dinged me for working from home last weekend." He would have been content to let it go at that, but William pushed to find out what had happened, and Ben found himself again defending his actions of the previous weekend, hoping that his climbing buddy would take his side.

"Sounds like Stephanie's advice was pretty good," said William. "Think about it from a climbing perspective. If I don't find a partner who has climbing values similar to mine, I just don't climb with them. Not only is it not fun, it's not safe."

Ben thought that was a little melodramatic; it's the level of skill that counts, not the value system.

"I climb because it brings me freedom and allows me to be curious, William continued. "If someone else had different priorities, such as getting to the top or climbing fast just for the bragging rights, I wouldn't want anything to do with them. In fact, you could say that the same principles of leadership apply to climbing: You have to know what you value and act accordingly. I value freedom and curiosity and the con-nection it brings with the people I climb with. That's what drives me."

"I guess I see what you mean," said Ben. "Only you've been climbing for ages, you've had time to figure this out, make a philosophy of it. I started being a leader a few weeks ago, and I haven't had a moment to breathe, let alone think about what drives me."

"The trick is to figure out what kind of leader you want to be," said William.

"Stephanie says that character brings credibility."

"OK, so what's your character when it comes to the office? Do you want to be the stereotypical hard-ass who doesn't care what anyone else is doing? Or do you want to be someone people look up to and say, 'I will follow that person anywhere?' I know which one I would choose."

Just then they heard a shout from the team above: "Climbing!" It was their signal to finally move off the exposed belay ledge of the fourth pitch.

"You're up," William said to Ben without hesitation, handing him the reins. "Have fun on this pitch. You'll love that rail."

And Ben did. He moved up and right along a beautiful three-inch crack, with a large overhang looming above his head and tiny wrinkles below for foot placement. As he peered down to the river 400 feet below, he realized that he too found freedom in climbing—although he'd never thought about it that way before. He certainly knew that he would follow William anywhere.

6 The Buddy System

Angela didn't sound like the bubbly young woman she'd been just a month ago.

"What's the matter?" asked Jen.

"I don't think I'll ever meet Ben's expectations," Angela fumed. "Look at this. I submit my status reports every Friday, and all they do is generate more questions. I haven't the foggiest idea what he wants from me."

Angela's frustration had been slowly brewing since shortly after her arrival at BCO-Tek, but this was the first time she had expressed it out loud.

"It's just his style," Jen reassured her. "Like yesterday, he went directly to the client to talk about my bug fixes instead of coming to me first. He's all action. I will say, though, that I was impressed when he wound up apologizing about that weekend he trotted in here like he was taking a break from sunbathing."

"Fine," said Angela, "but I wish we had more flexibility in how we do our jobs."

Ben had quickly developed a reputation as "taskmaster." The more stressful the job, the harder he drove them. From his perspective, it was an understandable way of trying to regain a sense of control. Kevin, for example, had been working with Ben long enough to know how to deal with it, by simply giving daily updates that satisfied Ben's need to be in the loop on key decisions. To Angela, though, Ben was quickly turning into a stereotypical micromanager.

If anything, Darryl was the opposite, but this proved no more effective. Over on the testing team, Darryl pulled everyone together for what he thought would be an exciting announcement. "Hey, guys? I came up with an idea that I wanted to share. I've been looking at some great online collaboration tools that are really going to help us all work more effectively together."

The response he got was far from the enthusiasm he had expected. "Uh, yeah," said one of them, "but I'm just wondering..."

"Yes?" Darryl pointed encouragingly to the team member. He prided himself on being the kind of leader who was genuinely interested in what his people had to say.

"It's just that we already have an e-mail program with plenty of utility for a four-person team."

"That's right," said Darryl, beaming. "This new tool will fit right in with it."

"We also have an online team chat room," offered another.

"And a discussion group," piped up someone else.

"Also, there's that project management tool you brought in last month, and the issues tracker we use every day."

Darryl was starting to feel deflated. "I don't really see the problem," he said, wishing he hadn't invited any feedback at all. They would love this new tool once it was implemented.

"If you really want to give us something new, we could use a new coffeemaker in the break room," said one of his team members. "Maybe one of those big pod things."

"Or an iPad for everyone would be nice."

"Man, that would be so cool!"

"OK, OK," said Darryl, trying to herd cats. "All very wonderful ideas, but this tool I'm talking about will let us update status, assign tasks to each other, and share documents."

"I get it," said the one who had asked for the pod coffeemaker. "This is so we can put information and stuff online in 'the cloud' instead of turning to the person three feet away and actually speaking to them."

Everyone laughed. Except Darryl. It wasn't fun to be struggling in his new role. He didn't want to impose on anyone, but he could feel this good quality of his being used against him as a sign that he was somehow weak. Lacking. He was only trying to be a thoughtful and considerate manager, and word was getting around that he was vague, that no one was clear about his expectations. He wondered what would have happened if he had just turned down the promotion. Would he have gotten fired? Or been able to return to his nice, comfortable life, doing his job well and not having people hate him so much?

A few minutes before noon, Ben was walking through the development team area and noticed that everyone had slipped out for lunch. There was a time when he would have gone with them, had a burger with his pals. He realized that it had been ages since they had invited him, even for coffee.

That's fine, he told himself. It's not as if he was lonely. He just happened to be wandering over by the test team area when he saw Darryl working by himself. "Hey, want to grab a sandwich?" said Ben, perhaps too eagerly.

Darryl snapped his laptop shut so fast he nearly caused it damage. "Sure," he said. "Where to?"

"Mexican good with you?"

"Yes. Absolutely. Love it," said Darryl, although he wasn't actually a fan. "Remember, we have to be back in time for our meeting with Stephanie, so we'd better get takeout."

They walked west two blocks down Pearl Street to a popular burrito joint. "So, hey," said Darryl while they waited for their order. "Are any of your team members acting weird?"

"Funny you should mention that," said Ben. "My guys are tiptoeing around like I've got bad breath or something."

"Yeah, me too," said Darryl. "Not bad breath, I mean they're acting funny. This morning I was updating them on this great new tool we're gonna use to track projects, and they started talking about iPads and coffeemakers."

Ben appeared to be studying the menu, as if he hadn't heard a word, which made Darryl nervous. "They're probably just intimidated now that we're team leaders, right?" said Darryl, trying to recover.

"Hmmm?" said Ben. Actually, he had heard every word, but Darryl was such a mess sometimes. Ben didn't want to appear equally vulnerable.

They took their burritos back to Stephanie's office, where each reported his team's recent accomplishments and his plans for the coming week. Then Stephanie asked a question that got Ben totally confused.

"How are things going for you guys?" she said.

Ben had just provided a well-reasoned report on his team's status, but perhaps Stephanie hadn't understood. "As I mentioned," he said carefully, "we'll hit our key milestones. Barely, but we'll finish."

"I'm not asking about your projects," Stephanie explained. "I meant, how is the transition to your role as team leader going?"

Ben and Darryl exchanged the briefest of glances. Had Stephanie been at Chipotle and overheard their conversation? *The woman has bionic ears,* Ben thought.

"Frankly, things are...different," said Ben. "Darryl and I were just discussing the subject. I've been working with Kevin for years, and with Angela and Jen and the others for some time now, and it's just, I don't know, *different.*"

Stephanie asked him to explain.

"Now that I'm in a leadership position, it's my job to make sure we're delivering this project on time, and I have high expectations," said Ben. "It's frustrating to have people who don't do things the way I like."

"Is that your experience too, Darryl?" asked Stephanie.

Darryl had been separating the lettuce shreds from the refried beans, but he quickly threw a napkin over his plate. "These were my friends," he said, "and now it's strange to be in a position where I have to direct them to do their jobs. For instance, I'm trying to do some new stuff, think outside the box, you know. And they're joking around and teasing me and not taking it seriously."

"I think I've got the picture," said Stephanie, nodding empathetically. "It's the transition between *being* a friend and *managing* that friend, isn't it? I remember when that first happened to me. I was a young lieutenant in the Army and was promoted to captain, and before I knew it one of my peers was my executive officer. We were heading out for a field exercise and he was responsible for the load plans in our trucks. When we were setting up our command post, all of our communications gear was in the back where we couldn't get to it immediately. The battalion commander dinged us for not having the post set up on time. It was difficult to be buds with this guy and also have to tell him what he did wrong, a definite strain on our relationship both personally and professionally, but we got through it."

"How'd you do it?" asked Ben.

"Carefully and intentionally. On one hand, I had to be courageous—making sure everyone knew my expectations and ensuring that I was making the tough decisions even in the face of resistance. At the same time, I had to be humble. My best advice is that your people want to see you as being human. They want to know that your ego isn't more important than their needs. Set the example in everything you do—just like we've talked about. Set clear expectations. Show them you care."

"I'm not sending them flowers, if that's what you have in mind," said Ben with a laugh.

Stephanie smiled. "There are other ways, you know. Check in on a regular basis. Be open and understanding. Create an environment where they feel their contributions matter. Does that help?"

"Sure," said Ben.

"Yup," said Darryl.

"Nice work, by the way," said Stephanie. "You guys are hitting your milestones on Q-Bank."

On their way out, Darryl opened the door and waved Ben through ahead of him. They gave each other a brief nod, then continued to their cubes, where each slumped in his chair, let out a sigh, and stared blankly at his screen.

7 A Long Lunch

Two weeks later, Ben was back to being completely focused on his work. The Q-Bank implementation was winding down, with AccuSave in ascendance. Things were really moving forward.

Outside Ben's office, the attitude was a little different. "This is never going to end," Jen complained to Angela. "We need more people if we're gonna get AccuSave live on time. Ben keeps agreeing to these ridiculous timelines without our input and expects us to deliver by working more hours. Q-Bank keeps passing right over Ben and calling me directly. I can't serve two masters."

"All I know is that he doesn't like me," said Angela.

"Who doesn't like you?"

"Ben. He doesn't say anything to me beyond asking about my progress. I'm trying my best, but it's just not good enough."

"I don't think it's that bad," said Jen. "I've worked with him longer. You have to remember, he's all about the business. It took him a year before he knew I lived a full hour away. It's been pretty rough pulling these hours and getting home so late."

"I don't know," said Angela in a voice of doom. "I'm still trying to figure out this P1 from yesterday. Uh-oh, speak of the devil."

Ben was on his way over to check on Angela's progress, or lack thereof. It was only the third time that day.

"Overheard you saying you can't get it right," said Ben. "Here, let me do it." He nudged Angela aside. He pulled up a command prompt screen, typed furiously until the keyboard almost caught fire, banged out a final "Enter," and announced: "Problem solved!"

"Um, thanks," said Angela.

Ben smiled and walked away, proud to have set the example again. Angela went back to her work without a clue as to what Ben just did, and wondered whatever happened to the confident woman with the bouncy step who had come here with such unbridled enthusiasm such a short time ago. It was really starting to bug her, but she couldn't quite pinpoint the source of her frustrations. She'd been having less enthusiasm for work and taking longer lunch breaks, and had less energy when she got home at night. Her favorite topic of late was "that manager guy." What she couldn't fully grasp just yet was that she still loved her work. It was "that manager guy" she couldn't bear. For now, everything about the job seemed to be shrouded in misery, and it was hard not to take that home.

8 The Town Hall Meeting

Ah, the town hall meeting. Sometimes called an all-staff. Otherwise known, in some institutions, as "nap time." Or the place where you first develop a dependence on antacids.

When Stephanie first took over as VP, one of her goals was to make the town hall meetings more interactive, or at least turn them into something you wouldn't mistake for The Dead Zone. She knew from previous experience that simply dumping information on attendees typically resulted in little more than silence during the meeting, while triggering rumors and questions in the hallways afterward. Instead of a positive experience, these meetings were often a breeding ground for distrust and resentment, because they reminded people they didn't really have a voice in anything that mattered.

One of Stephanie's first orders of business when she arrived at BCO-Tek was to hold a town hall meeting with the entire Professional Services organization every month. The difference was that she flavored them with the four ingredients of her Secret Sauce.

First, she found space where everyone could sit in a U-shape without the physical barriers of the typical conference room or lunchroom-style tables. Second, she asked team members to submit questions prior to the meeting, using a simple online survey that enabled them to submit anonymously if they so desired, while encouraging them to share their names, which they often did. This way, she could better tailor her responses. Third, she invited team members to give short presentations on various personal and professional topics. Giving center stage to people who were not in supervisory positions was critical to making the town halls work. Fourth, she followed up each meeting with action items, and asked for additional input to ensure that she captured what she heard. At the start of the next town hall, she would review the status of any open action items.

Using these four key steps wasn't the only way in which Stephanie showed that she valued her team. She was also a firm believer in transparency, and posted on her office window project status and performance metrics, whether positive or negative. This allowed everyone in the department to stay updated while demonstrating her openness and her willingness to take responsibility, all of which helped reduce barriers between Professional Services and the Sales, Engineering, and Finance Departments. Also, importantly, it allowed her to focus less during town hall meetings on project status and more on listening, gathering input, and recognizing everyone for their individual efforts and contributions.

In all these ways, Stephanie was able to develop a deeper level of engagement within the Professional Services organization. But nothing was as noticeably effective as her town meetings, and on this particular morning, at this particular meeting, everything was the same, except for Angela.

Until then, Angela had never spoken at a town hall meeting. This time, she raised her hand and stood. "I'm sorry, but could you clarify the next steps we have to take on Q-Bank?"

Ben could not believe his ears. After all he had done for her...like fixing that problem she had the other day, right on the spot. Having Angela voice confusion about something she should have known backward and forward from the beginning reflected poorly on Ben. Stephanie was paraphrasing Angela's question to make sure she understood, and opened the response to the entire group, but Ben was so enraged he thought his collar would burst, like The Hulk's. He hadn't known that Angela had it in for him like that, and tried to think back to the signs he must have missed.

"Angela, does that answer your question?" Stephanie was saying.

"Yes, thank you so much!" Angela was gushing. *What a phony,* Ben thought.

Meanwhile, Angela's heart was racing with fear. She had just gone over her boss's head...but she hoped he would understand. After all, the point of the town hall meetings was that everyone be heard, and *someone* had to let her know what was going on in very clear terms.

Ben and Darryl exchanged looks. Ben knew better than to roll his eyes, in case someone saw, but he didn't have a chance to because there was another hand up. This time, it was someone from Darryl's team. From across the room Ben thought he could see Darryl gulp.

"I wonder if you could also clarify...?" the questioner began, but Darryl couldn't hear. He felt as if he were underwater, with a glug-glug sound filling his ears. The woman asking the question was someone he had filled in on the same subject just last week. He hadn't actually spoken to her, but he had clearly laid out her responsibilities in the online collaboration tool. Had she lost her login name and password? *I'll straighten this out right away,* thought Darryl. *The minute I get back to my office, I am sending her a very, very detailed e-mail.*

"Good meeting, everyone, thanks," Stephanie was saying. As she walked past Ben and Darryl on the way out, she managed to keep her smile and to say in a pleasant voice, "You two. In my office."

9 Clarity and Its Discontents

There was no small talk. "Sounds like some of your folks need some very basic clarification on their roles," said Stephanie. "What do you think?"

Ben responded first, as usual. "I can't believe what I just heard in there," he said. "I have spoken to her about this at least three times already."

"Perhaps four times would be the charm," Stephanie replied. "Look, Ben, you have to keep in mind that Angela is not only new to the company, she's new to the workforce."

"Sure, but we still have deadlines we have to meet," Ben countered.

Stephanie turned to Darryl, a moment he never enjoyed. "How about you?" she asked him. "Sounds like you're in the same boat."

"Not really," he said. "The answer was very clearly outlined in the new collaboration tool we've been using. I assigned a task and due date, and provided some additional information. I even attached the design docs Ben created. Really, it couldn't have been more clear."

"It's clear when they're clear," said Stephanie. She sighed, and tried a different tack. "Remember the movie you guys went to see? Do you recall how Lieutenant Colonel Moore spent a lot of time with his battalion before deploying to Vietnam, getting them aligned around what they needed to do. Remember how focused he was on training his junior leaders?"

Two heads nodded glumly in unison.

"Part of what you need to do as team leaders is help get your people aligned," Stephanie continued.

"Aligned, right," said Darryl. "Uh, what does that really mean, though?"

"You have to get your people working on the right things. In Lieutenant Colonel Moore's situation, when people weren't focused on the right things, others died. Obviously the consequences for us aren't so dire, but they do result in wasted time and poor product quality. In the end, it's not just our clients who pay for it. So do we."

"Yeah, but Angela should have known what to do by now," Ben exploded. "Come on, she's seen the job description. She's been through the orientation. She's working side-by-side with Jen. I don't have time to babysit, you know."

"This isn't about babysitting, this is about leadership," said Stephanie. When she stood up and moved away from the glass table, Ben looked at Darryl and mouthed "whiteboard," and Darryl suppressed an urge to giggle. Stephanie erased something on the board from a previous meeting, chose a moss-green marker, and redrew the diagram with the concentric circles, "People" on the inside, "Lead by Example" on the outside. At the nine o'clock position on the outer circle, she added, "Align Your Team."

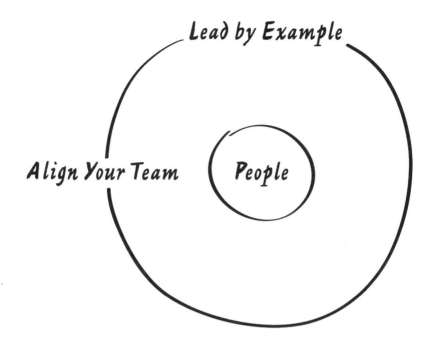

Lead by Example

Align Your Team   People

"One of your jobs as leaders is to get your team focused by aligning organizational goals with team and individual goals," she said. "If people are working on things that aren't directly linked with organizational and team goals, they're working on *the wrong things*, and we are just too busy here for that to happen. As leaders, you have to help people connect the big picture with their own role and their personal aspirations." She gestured toward the window near her office door. "Our goals are public. They're posted right here."

Darryl put two fingers on each temple and did an acupressure maneuver to ease his tension headache.

"Here's what I'd suggest," said Stephanie, "and this is similar to what you and I do together. Share these departmental goals with your people. Ben, ask Angela to develop her individual performance goals and standards based on these."

Ben groaned.

"She's going to need some coaching to get this right," Stephanie continued, "but have her at least begin the process so that she's invested and feels like she has a voice. Then meet with her. It may take a few times and certainly some negotiating and listening on your part. But review her goals, offer suggestions, have her make updates and then tweak them until they meet your expectations and they are exciting to Angela. This has to be a collaborative effort."

Darryl's mind was happily wandering off, since the conversation was really for Ben's benefit. *Using that collaboration tool was a smart move,* he thought. *Everything's laid out in plain sight.* At least today, he wasn't on the hook.

"And you, Darryl," said Stephanie, startling him into sitting up straighter and uncrossing his legs. "You'll have to do the same."

"Oh, I already have," he said, nodding vigorously. "I assign my team members tasks in our collaboration tool. They have these neat little colored tabs where you can click and..."

"Excuse me," said Stephanie, "but clarity doesn't materialize out of thin air. Using a tool is fine, but it doesn't take the place of actual, real-life, one-on-one conversations."

"Oh, boy," said Ben. "I guess I should have done this three months ago, huh?"

"Yup," said Stephanie. "This is important, guys. But it's never too late to clarify goals. Just start now. It's really hard to give people feedback throughout the year if they aren't clear on your expectations to begin with."

At the words "This is important, guys," Darryl had begun taking copious notes.

"OK, you've both got some work to do. By the way, Ben, a new developer just accepted our offer. His name is Henry, and he'll be coming on board next week. So, plan to go through the same process with him. You'll start fresh."

Darryl's note taking had subsided, and he was fidgeting. Stephanie asked him if there was anything on his mind.

"One of the things I'm struggling with is these people were my friends two months ago," said Darryl. "Now I'm responsible for their performance appraisals. It's just kinda weird."

"Yeah, for me too," said Ben. "No one laughed at my conflict resolution jokes last week."

Darryl wanted to point out that Ben's conflict resolution jokes weren't very funny, but he kept it to himself.

"This is a difficult transition for everyone," said Stephanie. "Leadership requires a balance of characteristics, with a lot of push and pull. You know how I said you have to balance courage with humility?" She went back to the whiteboard, chose a chestnut-colored marker, and wrote the two words in small letters below Lead by Example. "There are two more characteristics to balance. If you want to get your team aligned, you have to show a combination of being demanding and empathetic."

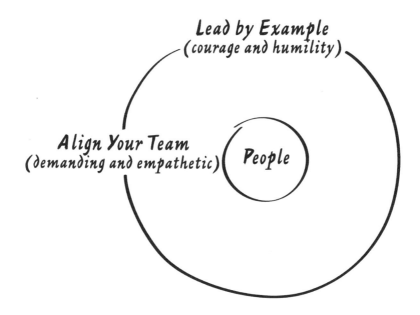

Lead by Example
(courage and humility)

Align Your Team
(demanding and empathetic) *People*

She wrote those words below Align Your Team on her model.

"Demanding sounds like a ruthless word, but what I mean is you have to set high expectations and hold people accountable to them. At the same time, you have to be empathetic, try to understand where people are and what they need. Having empathy is a critical component of building trust with your team members."

"At least it won't be as difficult with Henry, the new guy," said Ben, not quite getting the point. "I mean, it's not like we have a prior friendship."

"Actually, I'm friends with a lot of people I lead," Stephanie countered. "In fact, it helps me in many ways because I have a deeper understanding of their motivations and preferences and what they need as individuals to be successful. But I also balance that with being practical, fair, and aware of my behavior around them."

Ben and Darryl left Stephanie's office with a plan of action. They scheduled time with each person to review departmental and organizational goals. They gave their people a week or so to take a first cut at outlining individual goals. From there, they would review the goals together, and coach each person until individual goals were aligned with those of the team and organization. The process went fairly well. Within a day, Ben had met individually with Angela, Kevin, and Jen. He shared the departmental and organizational goals and talked about team purpose. They were surprisingly open to the process—even Kevin, who already knew exactly what he needed to do to be successful.

Ben found himself thinking about what Stephanie had said about balancing the characteristics of being demanding and empathetic. He caught himself a few times interrupting when people were talking about their goals. He'd have to remember to be more humble and give them a chance to speak.

A week passed. Ben met again with each one individually. Kevin's goals were pretty much right on, and in the course of a thirty-minute conversation they were able to agree on Kevin's plan for the year. Jen wasn't too far off, and with some minor changes hers would be ready by the end of the day.

As expected, Angela needed a little more coaching. Ben lost patience at times because it took her longer than the others, although he did note her enthusiasm for the process. He was determined to make sure he had a similar conversation with Henry on his first day. He wanted to get the new guy on track as soon as possible; their workload was too heavy for wasting time. With all the talk about goals behind him, Ben would be able to refocus on the Q-Bank implementation. *Man, all this stuff takes a lot of time,* he thought. He missed the time days when the only one he had to worry about was Ben.

Over on the testing team, Darryl realized he needed to add something more demanding to the equation. He had waited a week before beginning to meet with his team members, but it was finally done. He had asked them to "kinda take a stab" at creating their own performance goals. Darryl was happy that everyone now felt good about the process.

Another week passed before he met with each person to review the goals they had developed. As reluctant as he was to talk about friendship and being the boss, he got through it by being open and vulnerable. "This has been an awkward transition for me," he began. "You know, going from friend to being in charge. Here's how I see it. As a team leader, I'm being held to a certain level of standards by Stephanie, and it's also my job to do the same with my team. I'll commit to ensuring those expectations are clear. How does that sound? And I think we can be both friends and associates at work. In fact, that might help our relationship. By knowing more about you personally, I can better tailor how I lead this team."

With the goals conversations behind him, Darryl could refocus on Q-Bank. He breathed a sigh of relief. *I think people are beginning to enjoy having me as their leader,* he thought.

The workload remained heavy, but the team managed to push through it all. Stephanie was out of the office for the majority of that time visiting potential partners in India, meeting with customers, and taking a few personal days to spend time with her family. Before Ben or Darryl realized it, three weeks had slipped by without their regular meeting with her. The time had passed without incident, so both of them figured they could relax. Things were looking up.

10 Disciplinary Action

In the few weeks since Ben's goals discussion with Angela, she had made some initial improvement, but, to his bewilderment, he was still finding mistakes in her work that he felt she should have caught. *Gosh,* he thought, *how many times do I have to solve her problems for her?*

He wanted input about it from Stephanie, but she wasn't due back until the following week. Instead, he went down to Darryl's cube in search of a lunch partner.

"Burrito?" Ben said.

"Yeah, I need a break."

Once again, it was Chipotle, but they decided to dine there instead of taking it back to the office. "Angela's just not getting it," Ben said. "It looked good after our goals conversation. I thought things would change, but they haven't." He took a giant bite of his burrito, spilling black beans and corn salsa all over his lap.

"You know something?" said Darryl. "You're really a slob."

Ben ignored him. He slumped over the table, trying to hold the burrito together, and chewing like a gerbil.

"But I know what you mean," said Darryl. "I've got a similar situation with one of my team members. I suspect we might have to do something about it."

"Yup. It's time for a more serious conversation."

Ben decided he'd meet with Angela in person. Darryl had other plans. Either way, they agreed on one thing: Corrective action had to happen, even if Stephanie was still on another continent.

Before leaving the office that evening, Ben whipped off a meeting request to Angela for the next morning. Angela picked up the e-mail that evening on her corporate CrackBerry, and thought it was a very strange message indeed. Aside from their recent goal-setting session, Ben had never requested a meeting like this. It was scheduled for 9:30 a.m.

The next morning, Angela arrived early. She tried being productive, but it was impossible. She'd made the mistake of opening her e-mail program and every time the small blue reminder appeared in the lower right corner of her screen, she was drawn back into her inbox, abruptly abandoning the work she'd started.

Before she knew it, it was 9:30. She grabbed her notebook and stopped at the kitchen for a quick cup of tea before getting to her meeting with Ben slightly late, just as she had learned was customary at this company. But, atypically, Ben was already seated at the conference table, looking formal, with a single piece of paper in front of him.

In true form, Ben got straight to the point. No fluff. "This document outlines my concerns about your performance," he said. "Take a minute to read it, and sign at the bottom. This is a warning, Angela."

"What?" she said. "I don't understand. This is the first time I've heard any of this."

"I've corrected you five of the last six times you've come to me. I expect you to catch on."

"Wait, I don't agree with these allegations," she said. "Can I just take this back to my desk and read it more carefully?"

"No, you'll have to sign this incident report now," said Ben. "I also want you to sign a new job description." Ben pulled out another piece of paper.

"Am I losing my job?"

"No."

Angela was frightened and frustrated. "Well, if you're going to do this, can we at least agree to check in with each other a month from now?"

"Obviously there is some confusion," said Ben. "Go ahead and read your job description. If you need some clarification, let me know. And, yes, we can meet in a month. That's a good idea. But if you just do your job, you'll be OK."

Angela hardly had the bandwidth at the moment to take everything in, but she reluctantly signed the document, stood up, and walked out of the conference room without another word.

Over in the Testing Department, it was also not a great morning. Darryl had decided it would be best if he addressed the performance concerns he had with his problematic team member by e-mail. After all, he could outline his concerns so much better, and in much more detail, if he crafted them in writing. That way, there wouldn't be any question about his expectations.

Darryl had arrived that morning before anyone else, hoping to get ahead on his test scripts. Like clockwork, his team member arrived slightly before 9:00 a.m. Darryl peered at him out of his right eye when he came in and took a seat diagonally across in his cube. Darryl pretended to be deeply involved in his work so he wouldn't have to make eye contact with the team member, who dropped his coat on his chair, switched on his laptop, and wandered over to chat with one of the engineers.

Open your e-mail already, Darryl thought anxiously. This is killing me.

A few minutes later, the guy was back in his cube. As he double-clicked on his e-mail program, he glanced over at Darryl, whose eyes quickly shifted away.

It would be hard to miss Darryl's e-mail. It was highlighted with a red exclamation mark indicating Urgent, and came with a return receipt notification indicating that the sender would be notified when the e-mail was opened. Within a few moments, the team member understood why the boss had gone to all that trouble, because the message laid out all of Darryl's concerns in a very detailed and methodical manner. He was confused and taken aback. Why hadn't Darryl told him about this earlier? To make it worse, the last line of the message said a copy of the e-mail would be placed in his personnel file. He didn't even know he *had* a personnel file.

He walked over to Darryl's cube. "Do you have a minute? I don't understand this e-mail. Am I losing my job?"

"No, no, no, we wanted to give you some feedback on your performance," Darryl stated, using the royal "we" even though they were the only two people in the room.

"But this is the first time you've mentioned this."

"I e-mailed you several times on this subject and even updated your tasks on the collaboration tool," said Darryl. "You really should be doing this correctly by now."

"I don't agree with some of the items you listed."

"You'll be fine," Darryl said. "Just improve your attitude and it will make a difference. I also want you to sign a new job description. I think that will help both of us. Here, I'll e-mail it to you."

11 People Leave Managers

Jen was the first person Angela consulted, although "consulted" wasn't the right word. It was more like complained.

Angela's behavior was no longer subtle. She was just pissed, pure and simple. Over the next few days, at least half her time was spent planning her escape—from her boss. She reconnected with everyone she knew from school and took slightly longer lunch breaks than the slightly longer lunch breaks she had already been taking. Thanks to the apps on her phone, she was able to network with friends and business contacts on Facebook and LinkedIn without anyone in the office knowing. Within two weeks, she had two interviews lined up, one of which looked very promising.

She couldn't wait to get out of there.

Soon, she was ready for vengeance. It had been three weeks since her miserable meeting with Ben. The job at Hi-Tech wouldn't be as lucrative, but the work environment looked manageable. Anyway, Angela was ready to leave.

She arrived at close to 9:30 a.m. and walked right past Ben's desk. She knocked on Stephanie's door.

"Hi, Angela, come on in," said Stephanie. "Have a seat." It was the vice president's first day back from her long trip to India, and she was jet-lagged, but also jazzed.

Angela was nervous about once again going over the head of her boss. She was afraid it made her look unprofessional, but Stephanie had always been approachable—busy, like all the executives at BCO-Tek, but she always found a way to fit people in.

For twenty minutes, Angela poured her heart out, but there was nothing anyone could say or do at that point to make her stay. The best Angela could do was offer to stick around another two weeks, but they both agreed that today would be her last day. Stephanie would transition everything over to Jen.

Angela left Stephanie's office feeling younger, lighter, freer. Almost her old self again.

Meanwhile, a chat message from Stephanie popped up on Ben's computer screen: *See me in my office, please. STAT.*

"Well, the weary traveler returns!" Ben said heartily as he tapped on Stephanie's door and entered, although it was annoying to be dragged away from something he was in the middle of just like that.

"Have a seat, Ben," said Stephanie, not at all her usual affable self.

"Long flight, huh?"

"Not as long as it's been since our last meeting," she said. "I realize now that three weeks are way too long to go without our coaching sessions. That's my fault, and I apologize. It's easy for other pressing matters to get in the way, but coaching my people is also important."

"No worries," said Ben, putting his palms up. "Darryl and I have it under control."

"What happened with Angela while I was away?"

"Huh?" said Ben. "Oh, you mean...well, you'd be proud of me. I had to set and enforce a few parameters, and I handled it."

"You certainly did," said Stephanie. "Angela just gave me her notice."

"Her what?"

"Her *notice,* Ben. That's what it's called when someone leaves." She gave him a moment to let this sink in, and for her to pull back from the brink of sarcasm, which wouldn't be helpful under the circumstances. "Ben, Angela left because she was ticked off. She wasn't unprofessional, but she was pretty resentful. It sounded like the discipline process you put her through was the first time she had heard anything about your issues with her performance."

"But I've been asking her for the same thing for three months," Ben argued. "Nothing changed, not even after all those talks and aligning goals and whatnot."

"Did you give her any feedback along the way?"

"I gave her more than that," he said. "I've even showed her several times how to fix the issues she's been assigned."

"I think it's whiteboard time," said Stephanie. "Why don't you go and ask Darryl to come in here, too."

Minutes later, Ben and Darryl were back at the little round table in Stephanie's office, and Stephanie was back at her favorite place, in front of her whiteboard. Her leadership mural, as Ben liked to refer to it, was still there, untouched since she had been out of the country.

Stephanie pointed to Align Your Team in the nine o'clock position. "We talked about this the last two times we met, but the glue that keeps people aligned throughout the year is *feedback*. This is the courageous part I mentioned back in one of our discussions. No one likes to have difficult conversations with employees, but when we don't, we do a disservice to them, to the team as a whole, and to the entire organization."

Ben groaned, and Darryl felt bad for him. Ben had told him on their way to Stephanie's office about Angela quitting so suddenly. Darryl would have liked to tune right out and view this as Ben's problem, but he knew from experience that he wouldn't have been called in if it didn't affect him, too.

"Look, guys," Stephanie said kindly. "Feedback isn't meant to be punitive. It's designed to help people change their behaviors so they can improve and be successful in the workplace. If you do it correctly, you can still maintain or even enhance someone's self-esteem. That's important if you want them to be engaged in their work and committed to you as their leader."

"So, how should I have handled it differently?" asked Ben. "I wrote it down on the incident report and made her sign it so that I knew she understood what I was saying."

Stephanie saw this as a perfect *A-ha!* coaching moment. "Typically, having someone sign a written warning is one of the *last* steps in an escalating process," she said. "Never the *first* step. Before you ever get to that stage, you have to provide some coaching by being specific in your feedback and doing it in a timely manner."

"That's why I use e-mail," piped up Darryl. "You can get really specific when you write it in an e-mail. And it's very timely."

"No, Darryl," said Stephanie. "I'm sorry, but feedback needs to be handled in person. Face-to-face. Leader to team member."

Darryl's shoulders slumped with each mention of the thing he hated most: confrontation.

"By *specific,* I meant you should focus on the behaviors you want to see them change instead of on their attitude. When you say things like, 'You have a bad attitude,' it doesn't help anyone change. It's too vague. But when you cite specific behaviors that need changing, they'll have a better understanding of how to attack the problem."

Stephanie knew that differentiating behavior from attitude was a difficult concept for new leaders. She liked to explain it as a four-part process. "Here's a simple model for giving people feedback," she said.

"First, describe the situation or the behaviors you witnessed, and be as specific as possible. Next, describe the impact of those behaviors on you and on the team. After that, ask for input—get them to come up with ideas on how to improve. This gets them involved in the process and they'll be more committed to making the change. Finally, don't forget to follow up. Literally open your calendar and set a time to follow up with them, so you can reinforce the new behaviors. What gets scheduled gets done."

She looked from one to the other. "So, what do you think?" she said. "Situation, impact, input, follow-up. It's as simple as that."

"Um, sounds time consuming," said Darryl.

"Being a leader *is* time consuming. But this is part of what leaders do. They spend a good chunk of their time coaching and developing their direct reports."

The new team leaders nodded, and Stephanie continued. "If you don't do this, believe me, you will lose credibility. When leaders avoid having a difficult conversation, others on the team notice and they lose respect. I have seen this happen time and again."

"Time and again," murmured Darryl.

"The other thing I wanted to mention about feedback is that you have to *own* it. In other words, it should come from you and you alone. So own it by saying "I," not "we." Leaders take ownership of their words and their actions. They don't put it off on others."

"How am I supposed to remember all this?" asked Ben.

"Write it down. The next time you need to provide feedback, write it out head of time using the Situation-Impact-Input-Follow-up format I just showed you, so that your communication is intentional. Eventually the process will become second nature."

Darryl asked Stephanie to repeat the four steps slowly as he wrote them down.

"One last thing," she said. "As a frontline leader, you have a greater impact on your team members' job satisfaction and productivity and engagement than any other factor here at BCO-Tek. A report by Gartner Group said people don't leave organizations; they leave their supervisors and managers. I believe it. And I think now with Angela, you believe it, too."

Stephanie paused to let the point sink in. "This isn't just your fault," she said. "It's mine too. My job is to help you grow as leaders. But when we lose good people, it's a costly process, and we all feel it."

Darryl looked puzzled. "Costly?" he said, one eyebrow raised.

"By the time all is said and done, it can cost three times a person's salary to replace them," Stephanie explained. "It takes time and money to recruit new team members. There's lost productivity when an employee is physically here but mentally, and probably physically as well, looking for a new job. And it usually takes a new team member three to six months to get up to speed."

"Good grief," said Ben.

"Never underestimate the importance of your people," said Stephanie. "At the end of the day, having the right people on our team is our greatest asset."

12 Mind the Crevasse

After a week like that, Ben couldn't wait to go climbing. He and William had been talking for a while about climbing higher altitude peaks in South America, but for that, Ben would have to learn some new skills. Specifically, he'd have to learn about glacier travel. He had become a competent ice climber, and had spent plenty of time climbing steep snow, but learning how to move on glaciers was different. For one thing, glaciers have crevasses—large openings in the snowfield that could be several feet wide and up to one hundred feet or more deep. In the early season they were often covered with snow, and having the skills to navigate and cross these monsters would be critical to their success.

The snowpack in Colorado, unlike the Pacific Northwest of the United States, was quite thin, and year-round glaciers with large crevasses just didn't exist. So he and William decided to head up to a snowfield in the Indian Peaks, the mountain range in the western part of Boulder County that loomed above the foothills along the western edge of Boulder. There would be enough snow there, near the old mine just short of South Arapahoe Pass, to play on.

They started with some basic snow travel techniques. William taught Ben how to move across a glacier slope safely. Ben caught on quickly, although of course it would be more complicated once they were doing this at night, which was often the case on long summit attempts.

Then they worked on crevasse rescue. William shared a story about a climb in northern Patagonia on Mount Tronador, where he punched through a snow bridge while crossing a crevasse. Fortunately he was climbing with a competent guide and was arrested when he was only chest deep.

"Assuming one of our climbing partners has fallen into a crevasse, the first thing you want to do is transfer the rope's weight off of you and onto an anchor," explained William. "That way, you can build a haul system."

"Can't I just pull my partner out of the crevasse?"

"Not likely if they've fully fallen in. There's just too much friction on the rope across the snow, and the typical climber is just too heavy."

Ben started building his anchor, placing gear where he thought necessary. William stopped him. "The placement isn't deep enough," William pointed out. "As in, it won't handle the load. It'll pull right out of the snow."

"Yeah, but I'm just about hitting the ground," said Ben.

"OK, so what do you think you could do differently?"

"Well, let's see. I could use the picket and an ice screw, and then equalize the anchor across those two points, putting half the load at each point."

"Good thinking," said William. "What else could you do?"

They talked through a few more scenarios that could work. Every time they finished one, William would say, "OK, let's do it again."

Over the next several hours, William continued to guide Ben through tiny course corrections. He stopped him where appropriate, asked him questions about the impact of what he was doing, then asked him to think through ideas for potential solutions. Then they followed up and did it again.

At the start of that day, Ben was a beginner at building crevasse rescue systems. By the end of it, he was fairly competent. Enough so that William suggested they try something bigger on their next outing.

At around 1:00 p.m., dark clouds began building over the divide, so they decided to pack up and commence their three-mile descent. As they were hiking out, Ben thanked William from the heart. "I learned a lot today," he said, "and I'm stoked to get on the bigger peaks."

"You're the one who did all the work, my friend," said William.

"Yes, but it was your feedback..." Ben couldn't even finish his sentence. William hadn't taken on any additional work by solving Ben's problems. Instead, he had given Ben the gift of guidance. Feedback when he needed it. Had asked for input so that Ben could come up with his own solutions. Kept following up until Ben understood the task.

Thanks to William, Ben now had a whole new set of skills. He was ready to climb taller peaks, scale new heights. That wasn't what he had given Angela.

Chapter 12: Mind the Crevasse

Chapter

13 'People' First

Things seemed to be changing quickly. In just three months, Ben and Darryl had been promoted from consultants to team leaders. Angela had been hired and then quit. And now, here was Henry.

When Ben first saw Henry, he was caught off guard. The guy had to be in his midfifties. Everyone else on the team was in their twenties and thirties, with the exception of Stephanie, who was a fit and youthful forty-one.

One of these things is not like the others, Ben thought, the old *Sesame Street* song stuck in his head. *Get a hold of yourself, dude,* he told himself. He had to take this more seriously or he'd wind up with another Angela.

Ben welcomed Henry warmly. He took extra time to show him around the office, introducing him to the team in Professional Services, as well as the folks in Engineering and Marketing. Most of the salespeople worked remotely, so he had to make the introductions by phone.

"What are those posters up there?" Henry asked when they passed Stephanie's office.

"Stephanie is all about transparency. Those are basically our team guideposts. You know, organizational and departmental goals, team metrics, ground rules, roles, responsibilities."

"Well, that's interesting," said Henry. He seemed like a pretty calm guy. Ben hoped he'd be able to keep up.

"Thanks for showing me around," said Henry.

"My pleasure," said Ben. "I know you finish with orientation today, and you probably have a bunch of paperwork for Human Resources, so let's meet first thing tomorrow morning and we can discuss your goals and roles and responsibilities." Although Ben was still skeptical about having to spend so much of his time on the "people" aspect of his job, deep down he was still beating himself up over Angela's departure. What Stephanie had said about people leaving their managers, not their organizations, had hit him hard.

Later that day, Darryl and Ben met with Stephanie for their next one-on-one. They'd had to move them to Monday afternoons to accommodate a regular status update meeting with AccuSave representatives, since they were based on the East Coast and had a two-hour time difference.

Stephanie opened the meeting. "I know AccuSave is moving fast. How's it going?"

"Swamped already," said Ben. "Henry's first day with the team is tomorrow."

"Great," said Stephanie.

"Yeah, it'll be nice having another resource around."

"Another what?" asked Stephanie sharply.

"Resource," said Ben. "FTE." He used the acronym for full-time equivalent. "It's been pretty tough keeping up since, well, you know. Since Angela left."

"I can't stand those words—FTE, resources, head count," said Stephanie. "These are *human beings* we're talking about. Employees, team members, people. Not full-time equivalents. I think management uses those words because it enables them to make decisions without needing to take ownership or have the courage to see the people aspect of the equation."

"Ohh-kay," said Ben. He hadn't expected this tirade from the normally unflappable VP.

"Well think about it. If you want to implement a new process, you have to get people on board with the process first. If you want to change the direction of your organization or the culture, you have to get the people on your team to change first. It's so easy to slip into looking for technical solutions to our business problems and avoid the people side of the equation. It's a mistake, guys," Stephanie emphasized.

"I never thought about that." Ben said quietly.

"I believe that the most powerful and potentially effective tool we have for implementing our business strategy is our people. We have to put them first. As part of that, we have to think of them as *people*, not resources, FTEs, head counts, and nonexempts."

When Stephanie calmed down enough to give her an update on AccuSave. Darryl and Ben talked about last week's accomplishments, this week's plans, and what they needed from her. In general, Stephanie's goal was for them to do twice as much talking as she did, and in sessions where she was not holding forth on "people power," it worked.

Of course, there was always time for the whiteboard, whose "leadership mural" seemed to have taken up permanent residence. That gave Stephanie the rationale for putting in a second whiteboard. "How are you guys doing on the first two concepts we've talked about?" Stephanie asked them, indicating the phrases "Lead by Example" and "Align Your Team."

Darryl responded first this time. He raised his hand and bounced up and down in his seat as if to say, "Oh, oh, pick me."

"Yes, Darryl?" said Stephanie, amused.

"I'm doing great with that," said Darryl. "I'm thinking of every action I take in terms of leading by example."

Ben shrugged his shoulders. "I guess OK," he said. "I told Henry we'd meet tomorrow to talk about his goals for the year."

Stephanie looked at Darryl and asked whether he was consistently providing feedback for his team members.

"Sort of," he replied, with less enthusiasm than before.

"Guys, I can't stress this enough," said Stephanie. "This is one of the most important aspects of your job. When you see behavior you like, *recognize it.* It will reinforce the behavior. When you see behavior that isn't in line with what you expect, provide feedback. Just make sure you do it privately, OK?"

"Makes sense," said Darryl. "But I'm still struggling with it."

Stephanie sat back down at the table with them. "Have you ever been uncomfortable with me giving you feedback?" she asked.

Darryl looked puzzled. "I can't remember the last time you did," he said.

"I've been giving you feedback every Monday," said Stephanie. "What do you think these meetings are all about?"

"Oh, right," said Darryl.

"You see? Feedback doesn't have to be a big deal. In fact, an informal one-on-one like this is really quite effective, and generally leads to a constructive conversation. You should be doing this with each of your direct reports at least monthly. Put it on the calendar, or it won't get done. And one more thing, what's your plan for reviewing your team members' individual performance goals?"

"Well, now that everyone has goals, they'll be ready for their annual review when the time comes," Ben replied.

"Actually, Ben, in most companies, performance goals are pie in the sky. They're meaningless. And the reason is because they aren't reviewed throughout the year."

"Shouldn't they be taking personal responsibility for their goals?" asked Darryl, hoping to cut down on the number of one-on-ones in his future.

"Part of your job is to coach and help guide their performance, not just at the annual review but throughout the year," said Stephanie. "At a minimum, you should review performance goals once a quarter. Even better, pull them out at your monthly one-on-ones and there won't be any surprises at the end of the year. Which brings me to something else. This year, as a team leader, you'll be responsible for writing your team members' performance appraisals."

Ben wished he had a cold beer right now. All he needed was one more major task to add to his workload.

"One thing I like to do throughout the year is keep a log for each team member, where I jot down my observations of the individual's performance," said Stephanie. "One mistake leaders often make is not giving people a fair and balanced appraisal based on their performance throughout the course of the year. They tend to remember only the most recent things, or big things that stood out."

"You should teach at the University of Colorado," Ben said jokingly.

"I did during grad school," responded Stephanie.

"Right, of course you did."

14 Teamwork

Q-Bank was done. AccuSave was in full swing. Henry was settling in. Things were moving along.

Of course, AccuSave was quickly turning into a custom implementation, which was always more difficult than the standard projects. Ben already had a number of issues to deal with, and was bouncing among Engineering, Sales, and the client to make sure requirements were in line with the implementation efforts.

Fortunately, Kevin was the lead consultant on this implementation. He was now spending almost seventy-five percent of his time on the project team instead of the previously expected fifty percent. Henry and Jen were dedicated full time to the project.

Ben's weekly project team status meeting began six minutes after scheduled, and when he walked in, he started in the usual way. "Kevin, where are we?" he barked.

Kevin provided a concise update and hit all the key points, just the way he knew Ben liked it. When Ben turned to Henry and Jen, Henry went first. "I was working through the code the other day, and realized I didn't have the big picture of what the client is trying to do," said Henry. "So I went over to Engineering and talked with one of the guys over there. Hmm, what was his name? Bob. Yeah, Bob. And so Bob helped me work through the code line by line. But I realized I was missing a true understanding of our development standards. You know, things are different over here from what I'm used to."

Ben couldn't believe it, but Henry went on and on, talking about the differences in their development environment compared with his previous job, yadda yadda yadda. Finally, Henry appeared to come to the end of his remarks. "...But I'm still trying to get the marketing requirement documents from Engineering so that Darryl and his team can formalize the test plans."

Ben tuned back just in time to catch the last sentence, and said, "What's taking so long?"

"Oh, well, I've asked a few times, but I know they're really busy over there," said Henry.

"I'll take care of it and get those to you today," Ben said crisply as he made note of the action item.

Ben took back control of the meeting, directing the team on how things would unfold over the next week. It was going to be busy and everyone knew it, but there was a slight edge to Ben's tone that Henry didn't quite understand.

Over on the testing team, Darryl was also running his weekly team meeting, Darryl-style. "How's everyone doing?" he asked them. He liked to connect with everyone before getting down to business. By the time the actual meeting got started, it was almost fifteen minutes late. "So who'd like to go first?" Darryl asked, getting ready to start his usual round robin, where, one by one, he went around the table.

"OK, good work," he might respond as one team member finished and he'd get ready to move on to the next. "Keep plugging away. I know it's frustrating to work with Engineering sometimes, but we don't want to bug them too much. Just update the tracker when you get the documents."

He continued with the meeting, keeping the flow open and providing very little direction, hoping his team members would feel empowered to do their jobs. Or at least that's what he told himself.

The next two meetings proceeded in the same fashion for both Ben and Darryl's teams. On Ben's team, there were status updates from Kevin, then from Henry and Jen, then a directive from Ben on how things were going to happen that week. On Darryl's team there'd be an informal start, very little structure, and almost no support from Darryl himself. Walking out of the meeting, one of his team members thought to himself, I've seen it before. *Young managers reluctant to lead out of fear of not being accepted.*

Over on the development team, there was a major backward compatibility issue brewing. At their next meeting, Henry spoke up. "This is very similar to an issue we had at my old job. We were working on a similar platform, but with a few minor differences..." Ben couldn't believe that Henry went on for almost three more minutes of useless technical information. "...So, given all of that, all we need to do is reconfigure the last section of the code."

After all of that, the only thing Ben said was, "We got it covered," but Henry persisted. "The benefit of doing it this way is the added flexibility it provides during the implementation," he said. "I've seen it work."

"We just don't have time to deviate from the original plan," said Ben dismissively. He was so preoccupied with getting to his next meeting that he simply gathered his stuff without a formal wrap-up and walked away. For all he knew, Henry was still there talking.

Later, Henry and Jen were chatting as they walked back to their cubicles. "I'm telling you, this issue can be resolved differently and in the long run will be much better," Henry insisted.

"Ben's not much of an advice taker," Jen replied. "He's quick to shell it out, but short on listening,"

Henry had seen this before too—the young manager reluctant to lead his team for fear of losing control. It was easier to do it all himself than to delegate and trust others.

15 Time Management...*Not*

The AccuSave project was unique in that it had higher visibility than any other project completed to date by BCO-Tek. This was good and bad. Because it was a challenging project, it was the place to advance your career and learn about cutting-edge technologies. However, as with any project in the spotlight, it might quickly draw management's attention, which usually resulted in more work than seemed necessary.

Nevertheless, the team was getting the job done—just not always in the most efficient way possible.

It wasn't so much that the team members were bickering and fighting. It was quite the opposite. On the surface, people seemed to get along just fine, but they tended to focus on their own work without considering how it affected the work of others. For example, Kevin revised the project plan to accommodate a change from the AccuSave project team, and it was almost a week before Henry and Jen were informed.

"Kevin, that change affects almost every line of code we have created to date," Henry complained. "That's a lot of rework we need to do."

"We have to get this done," Kevin responded. "Management approved the change request, and it has a ton of visibility."

"We'll make the changes, but we'll be pulling some late nights to get ready for the first test run by next week. A little help would be appreciated," Henry said before he walked away.

The weekly staff meeting kicked off the usual way. Despite the fact that Henry had only been on board for about a month, he was getting comfortable with the team. He was far enough along in his career that he had no problem expressing his opinions, especially to the three "youngsters," as he liked to call them.

"Guys, listen," said Henry. "We're running behind because we aren't hearing about changes until after they're made. Most of the time, these change requests have an impact on our work."

"What do you need, Henry?" Ben asked.

"More time."

"It's not there," said Ben. "We have to meet the milestones."

"Well, then, how can we get more done in less time?" Henry asked.

"I have a few ideas," said Jen. "They're pretty basic, but I think they'll help." She went on to talk about some time management techniques she had learned from Darryl's team to more effectively manage communications over e-mail, track bugs in the system, and keep meetings focused and on track.

"You're not talking about Darryl's beloved collaboration tool, are you?" asked Ben.

"Yes, as a matter of fact I am," said Jen. "Darryl said it's working out great."

"Fine, then," said Ben. "Let's try it out."

They were all missing the point. It wasn't just about making incremental improvements in how they managed their time. Anyway, their schedules kept slipping. When things go awry in a software company, they escalate...to executive management. And when executives try to play project manager, things can get ugly, fast.

It began with Stephanie. She tried to handle an issue during a conference call with the client's project sponsor and BCO-Tek's CEO. Within minutes, Stephanie was trying to respond to questions that were beyond her knowledge. How could it be otherwise? AccuSave was one of almost fifteen client engagements in the pipeline. She'd have to get back to the CEO and project sponsor with answers.

The first person she went to was Ben. Earlier in her career, she might have gone directly to Kevin, Henry, and Jen, but she quickly learned why that approach would do more to undermine her junior leader's authority than anything else. There were short-term benefits to getting an answer more quickly, and people felt important when initially approached by an executive, but micromanaging Ben's project was not the right course of action.

"Ben, I had a meeting with the CEO this morning and I need to get back to him ASAP with the latest on AccuSave," Stephanie said, and followed up with a series of questions to get exactly the answers the CEO needed. Ben explained that stabilizing the code was taking longer because of last-minute changes AccuSave had requested. As a result, they were working overtime to get everything ready for next week's first round of testing. As consolation, he mentioned they had put in place a few of Jen's time management ideas that she had gotten from Darryl.

Stephanie's tone sharpened. Her words became more direct. "This isn't about time management. This is about cohesion."

"Maybe Darryl's collaboration tool will help," Ben responded.

Just then, Darryl popped his head in the doorway of Stephanie's office. "Did someone call me?" he said.

"Your timing is perfect," said Stephanie. "Remember when I told you that one of your roles as leaders was to align your teams?" The team leaders nodded in agreement.

"Aligning your team is about influencing people to work on the right things. Your next job is to actually get them to work on those things...*together*. This is all about cohesion. When a team is cohesive, its members collaborate and create efficiently. One of the mistakes leaders often make is they look to time management techniques to figure out how to be more efficient, once again overlooking the people aspect of the equation. I'm not saying to put away the calendars and project plans, but focus on the way your team communicates and interacts. Get people working *with* instead of *against* each other. They'll be a lot more productive."

As Stephanie was about to continue, she received a text from the CEO asking for the AccuSave info. "We'll continue this tomorrow," she told Ben and Darryl before hurrying off to placate the CEO.

Unfortunately for Ben, waiting another day wouldn't help. Things seemed to be escalating out of control. The more stressful it got, the more people would focus on their own work so that they could meet the team's milestones. This individualistic preference went almost unnoticed when the workload was low, but now with the added pressure, things were coming to a boil. On top of which, no one had the time to figure out how to work more effectively with the others. Everyone just had too much to do. Through no fault of his own, Kevin had missed an issues call with AccuSave, which forced Henry and Jen to fend for themselves. Things were going smoothly until an issue was brought up that Henry hadn't heard about. He said he'd talk to Kevin after the meeting and get back to them.

Why hadn't Kevin shared this issue with us? Henry wondered. *He knows we need to hear about changes as soon as they're agreed upon. We just talked about this last week.*

16 | The Shift

So, where'd we leave off, guys?" Stephanie asked.

"Collaboration trumps time management," said Ben wearily. "Or something like that."

"Oh, right!" said Stephanie, brightening. She went back to the diagram on her whiteboard. "As a leader, it's not enough to just to get your people working on the right things. You have to get them working on the right things...*together*. If alignment is about being effective, cohesion is about being efficient." With a cinnamon marker, she wrote "Build Cohesion" at six o'clock on the outer circle.

"OK, I got all that, but this people stuff is just taking so much time." Stephanie was surprised to hear this response come out of Darryl's mouth, not Ben's.

"Well, the job only gets done with people," she countered. "And if you want to get it done efficiently, your people have to be able to work together."

"Yeah, but we can't *make* them work together," muttered Ben.

"True," Stephanie agreed. "You can't *make* people do *anything*. They have to choose to do it. Like in the movie you saw. What did that leader do to inspire cohesion with his people?"

"There was that scene on the battlefield where one of the platoon leaders was trying to be a hero, but he got his entire platoon trapped instead," offered Darryl.

"That's right," said Stephanie. "He put everyone at risk without thinking through the impact his actions would have. As a leader, you have to create an environment where people think not only about what they're doing, but how what they're doing affects what everyone else is doing. For that, you need a team culture based on respect and trust. Without respect you can't have trust, and without trust you just muddle through from day to day, wasting all sorts of time and emotional energy."

"I don't know," said Ben, shaking his head. "It *sounds* like a nice idea, but let's face it, everyone on a team is really different. I mean, Henry's older than everyone else and, no offense, but it takes him forever to make his point. Kevin is detail-oriented and needs all the facts before he can make a decision. Jen's very quiet, very inside her head, and she's not letting anyone see the process in there as it happens."

"That's the point," said Stephanie. "It's through those differences that you'll come up with the best ideas and be able to capitalize on each person's strengths. If everyone thought the same way, no one would really be thinking at all."

"So where's the cohesion?" asked Darryl, leaning forward as if Stephanie had the Holy Grail, or at least knew how to draw one on a whiteboard.

"For all those differences to work on a team, everyone has to be able to appreciate those differences and understand how to leverage them."

"Leverage would be great, someday," said Ben. "Right now I don't need leverage, I need people who can keep up."

Stephanie wanted to shake him by the shoulders, but that didn't fit anywhere in the leadership model she was trying to teach him, so she took a deep breath and decided to offer concrete examples and suggestions. She talked about the importance of creating an environment of open communication where people can share ideas, debate issues, and approach each other when they need something. She explained that sometimes it takes longer up front, but when people are involved in the process, they tend to be more committed to decisions and to the team direction. In the end, it saves time.

"You guys set the tone, and everyone will follow," she explained. "In fact, what you do will get repeated by everyone else—regardless of whether it's good or not. If you encourage discussion, ask for input, and get people involved, others will do the same. It all starts with you."

"It all starts with me," Darryl repeated under his breath as he took notes. He hadn't realized he was speaking out loud until he heard his own voice.

"You mentioned that everyone has to, you know, celebrate each other's differences, raise a glass to them or whatever," said Ben. "How do we do that? And, uh, why?"

Stephanie chuckled. "I don't think I used the word 'celebrate,' but OK, everyone needs a better understanding of what everyone else brings to the table. It's not so everyone can feel warm and fuzzy about it. It's so they can learn to communicate in a way that works for the individual. As you know, a one-size-fits-all approach to communication isn't very effective."

"What if we're being very, very clear?" asked Darryl. "Isn't it up to the team members to be able to take that information and run with it?"

"Let's be real, guys," said Stephanie. "The two of you value being fast-paced and independent. You make quick decisions. You thrive in an environment of change. You're also both very competitive, in your own ways."

She looked at Darryl. "Now you, Darryl, I've heard you say many times that you take a hands-off approach. You also have a tendency to be less assertive, and you prefer an environment where you can support your people."

Stephanie turned to look at Ben, who put up a hand. "Don't say it," he said, and Stephanie smiled. "Yes, Ben, I'm going to mention Angela, just as an example. Her style was all about connecting with people. She wanted and needed approval and feedback, and she didn't get it. What mattered to her was working with others and getting the job done together with them. Our styles are all different. It's not a case of right or wrong. As leaders we have to be able to adapt how we interact with others based on what they need as individuals, and we have to get our team members to think about how their own styles affect each other so that they can do the same."

"Huh," said Ben. "I never really thought about it that way."

"Me neither," Darryl added.

"Most leaders don't," said Stephanie. "The good ones do."

The time seemed right for Stephanie to tell them about DiSC©, the behavioral-style profile tool she'd recently been using with the management team. She told them she'd arrange for Ben and Darryl's teams to walk through the process. Meanwhile, she asked what they thought they could do to start encouraging an open climate of communication.

"I can start with my weekly status meetings," said Darryl. "They tend to be pretty much the same thing every week."

"I can begin by asking more questions," said Ben. "And, believe it or not, there may just be room for improvement in my listening skills."

"No," said Darryl teasingly.

"Meetings are the perfect place to start," said Stephanie. She gave them some pointers on getting their team members involved in problem solving. "They're closest to the issues anyway, and when they see that you value their ideas and input, they'll be more engaged in the project."

She also advised them to spend less time on status updates during meetings, and more time on solving real problems. "You can update project status through e-mail, the intranet, status reports," she said.

"Even Darryl's collaboration tool," said Ben.

"Yes, even that," said Stephanie, and all three shared a laugh. "Just remember, *people first.* That's the key to our success."

Ben's next staff meeting started off as usual, when all of a sudden he asked a question. Not just any question, either. He asked everyone on the team for input. "Do you guys have any ideas on how we can work to resolve these latest issues with AccuSave?"

Kevin, Jen, and Henry all looked at each other, speechless. Jen suppressed a gasp. Kevin had an out-of-body experience for a moment during which he thought that maybe he had nodded off and wasn't fully awake yet, so had probably missed something. Henry took off his glasses and blew some nonexistent dust off the lenses to hide the fact that he was smiling.

Meanwhile, Ben could hear the crickets chirping. Uncomfortable with the silence, he cleared his throat. "I know I haven't done a good job in the past few months of asking for your input," he said with a wry smile. "I'm tryin' here."

"I think we can probably improve how we communicate," said Kevin. "It seems like things just get buried, and I'll be the first to admit I'm part of the problem. Between six or seven meetings per day, seventy-five percent on this project and twenty-five percent on the other two, I'm probably dropping the ball."

"Kevin, we all have a part in this," said Henry. "Hey, I have an idea. How about you include Jen or me in those change-request meetings? We can get a jump-start on modifying the code. It would buy us several days and we'd be more likely to meet our deadlines."

Ben was truly impressed. Why hadn't *he* thought of it?

"Works for me," Kevin agreed.

"Great," said Ben. "Jen, what do you think?"

Her eyes widened. This was a first. "Well, one thing we could do is a code review for major P1 issues," she suggested. "That would give us another pair of eyes on them to make sure we aren't missing any key requirements. It might take a few extra minutes of Kevin's time up-front, but I think it would save us hours in potential delays."

"Sure," said Kevin. "Just give me a heads-up a few days in advance so I can plan for it."

Already they had two potential solutions from this meeting that didn't originate with the team leader. Ben was starting to see the value of this method. "One more thing I want to try," he said. "From now on let's update the status reports on Friday afternoons. That way, everyone can read it prior to this meeting and be prepared to discuss high-priority issues, escalation items, and support we need from each other. What do you think?" He looked around for responses.

"Hey, anything to shorten this meeting," joked Kevin.

"I can't promise the meetings will get shorter, but they'll be focused on solving problems instead of delivering stuff we can read over e-mail."

They mumbled in agreement, and were pleasantly surprised by the lack of anxiety they felt as they left the conference room together.

Over on the testing team, Darryl also began his meeting in his usual way—by asking questions so he could gather everyone's input. But he too did something different this time. He followed up with more assertive questions, such as, "When can you commit to getting that done?" and "What support do you need from me?" He ended the meeting with: "There's one more thing I'd like to try. How about if we summarize all the action items we've committed to and then open next time with a quick review of them?"

Everyone looked at each other in astonishment, as if to say, "Who *is* that masked man?"

Chapter
17 Cohesion

True to her word, Stephanie arranged for a facilitator to administer the DiSC© profile to the teams. Earlier, they had taken the profile online—it took under fifteen minutes to complete—allowing them to analyze their collective data, team strengths, and blind spots based on tendencies of individual team members. Ben caught up with Darryl in the hallway afterward and expressed his doubts. "It seems about as scientific as astrology," he said. "Anyway, the last thing I need is to be boxed in."

"Yeah, I hear ya," said Darryl. "What if my people find out that my stars aren't in alignment? I'm not sure I want them to discover certain things about me."

When the day arrived, the facilitator made it clear up-front that the profile wasn't meant to pigeonhole anyone. Instead, it was designed to help people learn more about themselves and others, to be a framework in which to better understand people. He handed out everyone's results and walked them through an interactive process of understanding their individual styles. One exercise had them walk around the room according to different words that might describe their behaviors in the workplace. For example, some people moved to "active, fast-paced, bold," others to "moderate-paced, methodical, calm."

Ben was surprised by how accurately the profile described his style. "Wow, just looking at this helps me understand you," Jen told him. "For the past two years, I thought you didn't like me. Now I can see how it has nothing to do with that."

Across the room, one of Darryl's team members was also having an *A-ha!* moment. "Darryl, I think I've been making some incorrect assumptions about you. All this time, I thought you were uninterested in my work. Now I realize you were probably just trying to be supportive by acting hands-off."

Everyone walked away from the session wiser. Ben learned that it was his natural preference to be skeptical...but he wasn't sure he believed it. Darryl learned that it was his natural preference to want to be accepted by others; he just hoped people wouldn't think less of him for it.

The team leaders met with their vice president a few days later. "So, what did you think?" Stephanie asked.

"I was surprised," said Ben. "In a good way. You know, it's interesting. Henry and Jen both like to have really clear performance expectations, and when changes come down the pipeline they work best when I give them as much information about the plan as possible. With Kevin, I already knew that he's a detail-oriented guy, but I didn't really get how important it was for him to do things accurately."

"What did you learn about yourself?" Stephanie asked him.

"I learned that I prefer to work at a fast pace; I thrive on challenge and change; I tend to make decisions quickly," Ben responded. "Also, I'm motivated by control and authority."

"Duh," said Darryl.

Stephanie smiled, but she always made it a point not to pigeonhole people by their DiSC© style.

Darryl reported that he preferred to work with his people in a collaborative and supportive way, that he tended to avoid conflict, and that he wanted people to get along. "I also recognized that my tendency is to work in a more methodical fashion," he added.

Stephanie asked them to consider how their styles affected the people around them. Ben acknowledged that his tendency toward being fast-paced and quick to make decisions often didn't give people enough time to process information before they responded. As a result, they frequently didn't contribute in meetings. "We decided that I would prepare an agenda and send it out twenty-four hours prior to the weekly meeting so that people can arrive more prepared and ready to contribute."

"It was loud and clear that I avoid conflict," Darryl admitted. "And by conflict, I mean any uncomfortable conversation. People said they'd prefer it if I dealt with things head-on."

Stephanie was aware of Darryl's misery, but reassured him that as a leader, it was critical for him to build a strong sense of self-awareness as the first step in alleviating these problems. "This is what they mean by 'emotional intelligence,' and it's an aspect of leadership that is too often overlooked. I see too many leaders walking around without a clue." She turned to Ben.

"Oh no," he said. "I know that look. You're about to bring up Angela again."

"Sorry, Ben, but it's an excellent example of what we're talking about. Angela left in part because you and I didn't recognize what effect our styles had on her, and we didn't do enough to meet her individual needs. Remember, as a front-line leader, you affect level of engagement, morale, productivity, and job satisfaction more than any other factor here at BCO-Tek."

Stephanie went to the whiteboard. "Hmm, which one haven't I used?" she muttered as she pondered the tray of markers.

"Burnt sienna?" offered Darryl.

"Burnt sienna it shall be," she said, and wrote "vulnerability" and "drive" beneath "Build Cohesion" at six o'clock. "There are two additional opposing characteristics that leaders need to be effective. Being driven enables them to focus on and achieve team results. Balancing that with vulnerability enables them to create an open environment of communication and build trust."

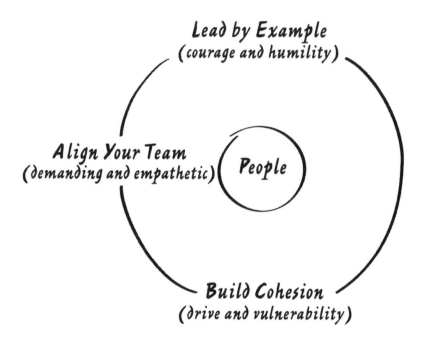

She suggested another exercise they could run with their teams that "will help take cohesion to another level." Before their next team meeting, they were to ask their members to think about what they needed from each other to be most effective and about what frustrated them most. "Then," Stephanie said, "have them share their thoughts with the rest of the team. Because, you see, it's all about..."

"Yeah, we know," said Darryl. "Putting people first."

18 | Momentum

Ben and Darryl had begun to leverage key lessons learned from each other. Darryl adopted Ben's meeting format, shifting to a focus on solving problems. Ben adopted Darryl's idea of ending meetings with a summary of action items and starting the next meeting by reviewing them. The only modification Ben made was to have everyone update the status of their action items on the shared drive, so they focused on reviewing only those items that were critical or that required additional discussion.

The week flew by, and suddenly it was Friday. Time to update their projects for everyone to see. Time for Happy Hour. This time, they'd actually get to the bar early enough for Happy Hour pricing to still be in effect.

Also, this time, Ben and Darryl were invited along.

On Monday morning, everyone read their team members' project updates in less than ten minutes. At Ben's team meeting, he asked what everyone thought of the DiSC© sessions. After some discussion, he assigned them Stephanie's reflection exercise. As Ben moved along with his new meeting format, he found that instead of spending time just dumping information on each other, they were actually solving problems...together. He was talking less and facilitating more. When he hadn't heard anything from Jen, he made sure to ask for her thoughts on the problem under discussion. Her thoughts included yet another brilliant idea, which reminded Ben that sometimes the quietest people had the most innovative contribution. It was his job to help bring it out of them.

Both Ben and Darryl felt like they were getting into the leadership groove, and actually caught themselves enjoying being managers.

The team leaders had begun monthly one-on-ones with their direct reports, just as Stephanie had suggested. Their team members even welcomed the idea of reviewing their performance goals once a month. Both Ben and Darryl were getting better at providing feedback, and found that when they did it consistently and with the Situation-Impact-Input-Follow-up format Stephanie had given them, people took the feedback constructively and rarely became defensive or distraught.

Both teams continued to build momentum. At Jen's suggestion, they changed the Monday meeting name from "Status Meeting" to "Solutions Meeting." At the next one, Ben kicked off the exercise based on the DiSC© assessments. "I've prepared a simple worksheet for taking notes," said Ben. "As you hear each person tell us what they need and what frustrates them, write down your observations."

They began, one after the other, sharing what they needed from each other and what was in their way. Ben went first, although it made him feel vulnerable, and by leading by example and setting the tone, he encouraged others to follow. Everyone walked away with a better understanding of each other. It was clear that they all wanted to be successful; they just had to learn to leverage each other's strengths to make it happen.

"I think we should do this whenever a new team member comes on board," Kevin suggested.

After the meeting concluded, Ben found himself thinking about what he'd heard from everyone and the differences in their needs. Kevin wanted details. Specifically, he said, "If you don't come to me with the details, I'll send you back." Credibility to Kevin was about doing things the right way with quality in mind, and taking a logical approach with the facts to support it.

Henry, on the other hand, said he appreciated having time to reflect on questions. *It's not that he talks too much,* Ben thought. *He just prefers to make sure all the bases are covered. When I don't give him time to process information before contributing, he's forced to do that on the fly and it comes across as being unprepared and verbose.*

Team members agreed that in addition to publishing an agenda, if Ben needed a decision, he would get a pre-read out to everyone so the processing could begin prior to the meeting. Henry also agreed that if he needed more time to process information before contributing, he would ask for it and then commit to responding back to the team within a few hours.

Jen said she enjoyed working independently. *It's not that she's quiet and doesn't want to contribute,* Ben thought, *she just values having clear performance expectations and then working autonomously.* She asked for some of the same things as Henry, and also requested detail-oriented and structured work.

Finally, Ben asked that people communicate with him concisely. He noted his preference for bullet-point e-mails rather than short stories he would never read.

The key was to keep this positive momentum moving forward. The question was...how?

19 Skywalker

Colorado has a very dangerous snowpack. Snowfall builds on weak layers formed in the early season and eventually large sections release. Avalanches claim the lives of about six people each year. In the late spring and into early summer, however, the snowpack layers begin to consolidate and gain stability. That's the best time to climb the couloirs, the narrow snow chutes that form on the side of some of the steepest peaks in the Colorado Rockies.

It was good timing for William and Ben to perfect their snow-climbing techniques. They'd have to start getting on steeper and more committing routes if they wanted to be ready for their trip to Ecuador in the fall.

They picked a route called Skywalker Couloir on the west side of the 13,397-foot South Arapahoe Peak. It was a narrow chute, angled at a steep sixty-five degrees, with large granite walls on either side. Climbing the route safely required that they begin before the warmth of the sun created instability in the snowpack, so they decided to meet in the Safeway supermarket parking lot at 4:00 a.m. That would put them at the trailhead by 5:00, at the base of the route by 6:30, and at the summit around 10:00 a.m. If all went well, they'd be back to the car by 11:30 and in Boulder before most people were having lunch.

That was the plan, anyway.

"You're late," said William sternly.

"Good morning sunshine to you, too," replied Ben.

"Fifteen minutes might not mean a lot in your regular world, but if you want to be prepared for the bigger peaks in Ecuador, you have to get serious. Over there, 4:00 a.m. is a luxury. We'll be starting at 1:30 a.m."

Ben did a quick reality check and realized William wasn't kidding. "Sorry," he said. "I'll put my game face on."

"Put on whatever face you want, just be on time."

Ben grabbed his pack and mountaineering boots and placed them carefully in the back of William's Subaru Outback. He didn't want the ice tools attached to the back of his pack getting caught on the other gear back there.

They arrived at the trailhead somewhat later than they'd planned, and quickly pulled on their boots and gaiters to head up the trail. About an hour later they were at the base of the route where they each sat on a small boulder as they donned their crampons and strategized about the best way up. The climb was imposing, with about 800 vertical feet of steep snow, followed by a rocky scramble to the summit.

They roped up, and William set off first as Ben belayed.

After William ran the rope out about 200 feet, he set up an anchor and put Ben on belay. When Ben arrived at the belay station about ten minutes later, William asked, "How'd it go?"

"Pretty good," said Ben. "Ice climbing definitely makes the steep snow sections more comfortable."

"Do you mind if I give you some feedback?" asked William.

"Please do. I want to learn." *Feedback is all about learning,* Ben mused. *I'll bet my people want feedback from me, just like I want it from William.*

William gave Ben some ideas and pointers on improving technique while saving energy. "Which reminds me," he said. "When we're climbing in Ecuador, it's likely we won't be able to see or hear each other. We'll have to use rope signals."

They agreed to stick to techniques similar to the ones they used for rock climbing: Four tugs on the rope indicated that the lead climber was off belay; an additional four tugs meant that the lead climber had the second person on belay. They also discussed better ways of swapping gear between leads that would make the transition from lead climber to follower faster. "On our summit day in Ecuador, we'll have to cover 4,000-plus feet of vertical gain," William said in conclusion. "We'll need to be efficient. We'll need to be on the same page and work cohesively. Make sense?"

"So efficiency comes from cohesiveness," he said. "That's exactly what my vice president was telling me at work."

"Absolutely. If we want to be fast, we have to trust each other, understand each other, and work together."

As William and Ben continued climbing, they got smoother with each pitch. It suddenly hit home for Ben that shaving just a few minutes off each transition could save considerable time on a long and committing climb. Efficiency didn't only translate into speed. In the mountains, it translated into safety, too. Less exposure to the elements. Less exposure to degrading snow conditions and rock fall.

They finished the actual Skywalker Couloir via the Princess Leia route—the steepest part of the climb. "That was absolutely amazing," Ben exclaimed.

They went on to reach the summit. It was a beautiful day. More than anything else, Ben had an amazing feeling inside. A sense of accomplishment and contribution. A sense that he mattered. William's comment contributed to that: "Great job leading that last pitch," he said. "Nice work on the transitions, and I was glad to see how you remembered to modify your technique."

Later that night as Ben was still dreaming about the day, he couldn't get William's words out of his mind. He was fired up. Motivated.

20 | Motivation

"Here's a movie question for you," said Stephanie the next time Ben and Darryl met in her office for their weekly tune-up with her. "Why did that helicopter pilot in *We Were Soldiers* keep flying back into the combat zone to pick up the wounded and drop off supplies, even in the face of enemy fire? Even when the landing zones were shut down?"

"I don't know," said Darryl, "but that was some serious commitment."

"That's exactly right," said Stephanie. "Commitment. Our ultimate goal as leaders is to build a team that's committed. When people are committed to you as their leader, they'll go way beyond the call of duty to get the job done—not because they have to, but because they want to. On the other hand, if you marginalize people, you'll build a team that's merely compliant. They'll do only what they have to, to get by, and nothing more."

"OK, I'll bite," said Ben. "How do we build commitment?"

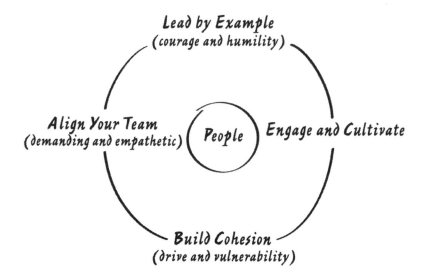

Lead by Example
(courage and humility)

Align Your Team
(demanding and empathetic)

People

Engage and Cultivate

Build Cohesion
(drive and vulnerability)

"Ah," said Stephanie. "That's the last piece of the puzzle." She went over to her whiteboard and rummaged for a maple marker with which to write "Engage and Cultivate" at the three o'clock position on the outer circle. "Commitment comes when we create a work environment that's rewarding for our people."

"We have to motivate them," Ben stated confidently.

"No, you can't motivate people," said Stephanie. "They can only motivate themselves. But as their leader you can create an environment that feels motivating to them."

"Sounds like an old Jedi mind trick," said Ben, cracking himself up.

"Pay attention, Luke," said Darryl.

"Think about the work you just did with DiSC© and that follow-up exercise. You learned something different about each person, and that they all want and need different things in their work environment."

"But how do we use that?" asked Ben.

"First, you can tailor how you recognize people. Recognition is a critical component of leadership and can help you build team member commitment. Second, if you understand what people aspire to and what's motivating to them, you can take your vision for your team and appeal to their individual aspirations."

"I don't have a vision for my team," Darryl admitted.

"Well, you *should*," said Stephanie. "It doesn't have to be complicated."

Both Ben and Darryl looked perplexed.

"Answer this question," Stephanie continued. "What's the best possible outcome your teams could achieve?"

Ben had a typically results-oriented answer at the ready. "We'd serve our clients and finish our projects on time and on budget."

"OK, not bad," said Stephanie. "You might also add a people aspect to it. Something like, 'while creating a team where people work hard and collaborate and have fun.' Now you'd have a great vision. You could use it in your one-on-ones and status meetings, and any time you interact with your team members. It solidifies your intent with the team."

"Sorry, we no longer hold status meetings," Ben interrupted. "They're *solutions* meetings."

"I have a question," said Darryl. "How do we know what kind of environment is motivating to our people?"

Stephanie responded, "Just ask."

21 What People Want

Ben had decided that in his next set of one-on-ones, he was going to ask his team members what motivated them and how they wanted to be recognized.

The results were astonishing.

It turned out that Henry lived for his grandkids. If there was an opportunity for recognition and reward, what he wanted most was time with family.

Jen had been studying Spanish at night. She loved learning about new cultures and her dream was to travel and see the world, so the best reward for her contributions would be time off, and maybe the opportunity to accrue reward points toward additional future vacation time.

Kevin was all about being challenged in his work. His career path came first, so recognition could be as simple as lunch with an executive or taking on a special assignment. Kevin was the logical choice for someday taking over Ben's role.

What struck Ben most was that none of them mentioned money—at least not as a primary motivator. It wasn't that they wouldn't appreciate a pay raise, but, given that they were fairly compensated compared to similar companies, there were other aspects of their work or what their work could do for them that turned them on more than money. Even Ben asking them about their aspirations and personal goals produced a sharp rise in enthusiasm: Their body language changed; their voices rose to a new pitch. "In almost thirty years in the workplace, you're the first manager to ask me that," Henry told him.

Ben was inspired by this new information, and surprised how little effort it took to understand his people at a deeper level. He felt there had to be more to this.

The following Monday, Stephanie noticed that Ben was looking ragged. "Tough training climb this weekend?" she asked sympathetically.

Ben raised his eyebrows. "Actually, no," he said. "I've been working on something."

"A master plan for the universe?"

"Well, something like that," he said with a grin. "It's definitely a plan, though. A reward and recognition plan."

"Sounds interesting," said Stephanie. "Got a few minutes to chat about it?"

They grabbed their coffees and took a seat. "It occurred to me that we busted butt all through Q-Bank, working long hours, nights, and weekends, and I never took the time to recognize my people for their efforts," said Ben. "You did, of course, at the town hall meetings, but I never did anything special."

Stephanie nodded, urging him on, but inwardly she had to smile. She had been telling Ben and Darryl that recognition was an important aspect of engaging and cultivating people, and now Ben was no longer just taking notes, he was attempting to put this concept into action—and that meant Stephanie had done her job well.

"I was trying to figure out how to determine what was motivating to my people," Ben continued. "I had the DiSC© information, but that didn't explain everything. For instance, ever since Henry came on board I've had the feeling that we weren't on the same wavelength. It didn't mean I couldn't work with him, but I never felt I understood him."

"You're absolutely right, Ben. One of the critical mistakes leaders make is that they don't get to know their people on a personal level. They draw a line in the sand between business and personal, and as a result they never learn anything meaningful about what each individual needs in order to be successful in the workplace. Because in real life, there's no such clear division between 'work,' where they spend their days, and 'personal,' which is who they are."

Ben agreed. "I won't be making that mistake again," he said. "I'd like to implement a recognition plan that combines a lot of the things you and I have talked about along with what I've been learning recently about my people. I think I can do some incredible things without spending too much money, although I may need some kind of a budget for this." He paused to see whether Stephanie was on board with the idea.

"OK, I'm intrigued," she said. "Tell me more."

Despite his exhaustion, Ben excitedly laid out the three-point plan he'd been devising. The first part was about creating goals at the beginning of the performance year, or as soon as a new team member comes on board, and reviewing them monthly. Making sure expectations are clearly understood. Providing feedback along the way. "I'm also working with them to create some team norms," he said. "I realized when I was climbing with William that it's more efficient and effective when we agree on some simple guidelines up-front."

The second part of the plan was to include personal goals in all goals discussions, and on a separate document to set out a plan for achieving them.

"Three...now here's the kicker," said Ben. "When people go above and beyond—either in achieving their work-related goals or exemplifying behaviors aligned with our team norms—I'll recognize them with rewards that are linked to their personal aspirations. I'll give you an example. Kevin is really focused on his career and wants to be a manager someday. So whenever he goes above and beyond, I'd like to allocate some funds for additional training or a conference he's interested in. Or we can look for additional opportunities for him to take on more leadership responsibilities."

Stephanie was quite enjoying herself, and for once didn't have to do all the talking.

Ben went on to describe the situation with Henry and his grandkids, where an extra day or two off would go a long way. "As for Jen, she wants to travel. We could give her Visa points or something that can be applied toward her travel budget, or maybe even pay for her Spanish lessons."

Stephanie liked what she heard. Her only caveat was that there be space for some kind of recognition on day-to-day items as well, even just praise, "as long as it's frequent, timely, and specific." She gave Ben the go-ahead on his plan. "Ben, you're really stepping up to the title of leader," she said, and Ben saw firsthand, in that moment, what some timely and specific praise could do for a person.

He began implementing his plan, using an estimated annual recognition budget of around $500 per person. What he would discover over the next few months was that the savings in productivity and engagement were at least fifty times the return on that investment. Not only did everyone feel appreciated, they also showed up just a little bit earlier and took more focused action in line with their goals and norms. Communication and teamwork improved. They took ownership of their work and followed through, especially when they handed off to another team member or department. Ben never would have imagined that something so simple and inexpensive could create such a huge impact.

His program didn't go unnoticed in the rest of the company. Stephanie was so impressed that she decided to implement it across the Professional Services organization. Within twelve months, turnover fell from close to twenty-five percent to eighteen percent. The $500 per person cost of the program was a small price to pay for the significant reduction in attrition costs, not to mention improved client service.

The benefits accrued in other ways as well. Over time Ben realized it wasn't just the recognition that excited people. The more he got his people involved, the more engaged they were. He began switching facilitators for the weekly solutions meeting, enabling each of his team members to truly be part of the meeting results. They took ownership of the new responsibility, and Ben gained a different perspective. He not only sat in a different seat at each meeting, he also played the role of participant. In this way, he began to see and appreciate his team members in a new light.

Chapter 21: What People Want

22 Delegate and Develop

All Ben wanted to talk about was his upcoming trip to Ecuador, and his excitement was contagious. So much so that Darryl actually said, "Ya know, I think I'd like to try climbing sometime." Thus was born a mini-team-building event.

It took a few weeks to organize, what with their busy schedules and tight deadlines, but the time finally arrived for Ben to take Darryl and Stephanie climbing. Ben knew that Stephanie was already a strong climber, but Darryl was a beginner who had only been to the climbing gym a few times. He knew how to belay, but didn't have any outdoors experience. Their goal was to climb the First Flatiron—one of the beautiful sandstone cliffs that dot the foothills of Boulder and that is in almost every picture and postcard featuring the town. Even though it was considered an easy climb overall, the committing 1,000-foot face often took beginners by surprise. It was a twenty-minute approach to get to the climb, eight long pitches of easy climbing, and then a thirty-minute hike back to the car. It would be a relatively long day.

At the base of the route, Stephanie asked Darryl to flake out the two climbing ropes. *Wow,* he thought. *She's the expert and she trusts me to do this. Feels good.* She watched him closely and gave him some pointers. By the end of the process, Darryl had learned some new skills in managing ropes.

The day went perfectly and the weather was clear. Stephanie and Ben switched leads on each pitch, and Darryl took ownership of carrying their one shared backpack and finding the trail for the hike out. He couldn't have been more excited. When they returned to the car, Darryl said, "That was amazing! Thanks, you guys. I learned a ton and I can't wait to do it again."

Ben and Darryl shook hands in a near high-five motion at chest level, pulled in close for their guy-hug, and smacked each other on the back. Stephanie smiled at the typical macho display.

Later that day, Darryl was still feeling the physical and emotional high of the whole experience. As he reflected on the climb, he realized that part of why he felt so good was the role Stephanie had enabled him to play from the beginning, and the added and unexpected responsibilities she and Ben handed him throughout their shared adventure.

I wonder if that same idea would get people motivated at work?

At the Monday morning team meeting, Darryl decided to hand off certain tasks to some of his team members. They were jobs he was comfortable doing himself, but they kept him trapped serving as a senior consultant instead of spending his time as a manager. He was happily surprised to see that everyone took hold of these new responsibilities with eagerness. When he and Ben were back in Stephanie's office for their weekly meeting, he was excited to share that delegating these tasks was a direct result of the weekend's climbing experience.

"That's right," said Stephanie. "When you delegate, it shows people you trust them. It gives them an opportunity to develop new skills, and frees you to do things you need to do as a manager—such as setting your vision, planning ahead, and dealing with higher-level customer issues."

She launched into a discussion of how to delegate tasks. Ben and Darryl hadn't realized there was an art to it.

"First, you need to adjust how and what you delegate to the skill level of your team members," she said, and looked over at Ben. "Kevin is very experienced. You can probably just give him an objective and he'll figure out the tasks he needs for achieving it. With someone less experienced, like Jen, you'll want to share your objectives and perhaps coach her on what tasks she'll need to do for completion. You'll absolutely have to check in with her along the way. Unless it's a birthday party, you don't want any big surprises."

"I *hate* surprise parties," mumbled Darryl, turning red just at the thought of his last one.

"Another consideration is the level of authority you're delegating along with your objective," Stephanie continued.

At the word "authority," Ben bristled. *I fight authority,* he said to himself. *Authority always wins.* "What do you mean here by authority?" he asked.

"Are you delegating just a task, or the actual ability to make a decision? With each person you should spell out what level of authority you're granting them. Again, it might look differently for each person, based on skill level."

Darryl jumped in to clarify. "Just to make sure I'm hearing you correctly, because I think I may need to redelegate what I just delegated this morning, let me see if I can rephrase. You're saying that the proper way to delegate is to share my intent, then ask for their input on the tasks they need to complete, and maybe do some additional coaching for less-experienced people. Next I decide on a milestone check-in for some people to make sure they're supported and on track, and then, as a fourth step, let them know the authority they have to make any decisions along the way?"

"You've got it," said Stephanie, beaming at him. "Provide your intent, get their input, agree on when to check in along the way, and clarify their authority level. The key step in there is getting their input. Again, involving them in the process builds engagement and cultivates their skills."

"I see," said Ben. "So I might ask Jen to provide me with options so I can make a decision, and I might empower Kevin to make decisions and just keep me informed?"

"Exactly," said Stephanie. "Good work today, gentlemen." As she ushered them to the door, she looked directly at Ben and said, "I didn't know you were a John Mellencamp fan."

"Huh?" he said. Both Stephanie and Darryl were laughing.

Oh God. Was I actually humming that out loud?

Chapter

23 The Motivation Debrief

There was time for only one last session with Stephanie before Ben took off for Ecuador, and he wanted to make sure he didn't miss anything important for the few weeks he'd be away. "Well, there's one last piece to Engage and Cultivate," said Stephanie, examining the model on her whiteboard. "It's simple, really. It's about encouraging learning and development."

She chose a mocha marker from her collection. "If we believe that having the right people on our teams is our greatest asset, and I certainly do, then we have to constantly be giving them the tools to do their job. The mistake many leaders make is that in tough economic times, the first item to get slashed is training, but whatever short-term budget relief they get is more than offset by longer-term gaps in skill and innovation. I've learned over the years that when we invest in our people, even when times are lean, they tend to stick around longer, stay engaged, and have higher levels of productivity."

"Makes sense," said Ben.

"Just as important, when people are learning new things, it allows them to think outside of the corporate box. Learning crushes complacency and inspires innovation. We want team members who look for newer and better ways of doing things, and who share their best ideas with us. Learning and development are the cornerstones of creating a sustainable competitive edge."

The three of them began to brainstorm ways to make this happen at BCO-Tek, where a relatively small Human Resources Department didn't necessarily mean they couldn't conduct training. They'd just need to get creative about it. They could use external trainers or internal subject matter experts. They could conduct monthly lunch-and-learns and encourage team members to seek out informal mentors. They also discussed setting up a budget for people to attend monthly association chapter meetings.

"To truly engage and cultivate team members, a leader has to balance a final set of opposing characteristics," said Stephanie, finally getting to use her mocha marker. Below Engage and Cultivate she wrote the words "consistency" and "curiosity." "On one hand, a leader has to be consistent by providing stability and vision for the team, especially in the face of change. On the other hand, the leader has to be curious—eager to grow and learn and be open to new ideas."

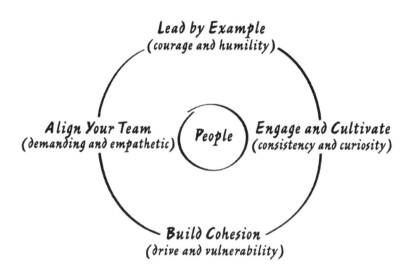

She looked back at the model and then at Ben and Darryl. "Well, there's the model," she said. "It's not rocket science. No silver bullets. Leadership is about doing basic things on a consistent basis, and if you do all of these things well, you'll be tremendously successful."

Ben and Darryl thanked her. She had no doubt that the two of them *would* be tremendously successful. "I'd like to keep these meetings going, but you guys have come so far that I think we can space them out to every three weeks," she said. "What do you think?"

They all pulled out their smart phones to reschedule the recurring meetings. As they were leaving Stephanie's office, Ben tried to get in the last word. "What are you going to do with all that extra whiteboard space now that you won't have us here on a weekly basis?"

Stephanie chuckled. "Go enjoy Ecuador," she said. "Climb safely."

24 A Higher Level

William and Ben landed in the capital city of Quito, with a sprawling population of more than 1.5 million. The city sits just twenty-five kilometers south of the equatorial line, yet enjoys a wonderful spring-like climate because of its elevation, 10,000 feet above sea level. In fact, Quito is the second-highest major metropolitan city in the world. Just being there helps mountaineers acclimatize during the week before attempting the big peaks.

After months of planning, the men had decided to attempt two main peaks as part of their expedition. The first would be Ecuador's third highest peak, Cayambe, which rose 18,991 feet above sea level. The second would be Cotopaxi, which stood at 19,347 feet. Both were significantly higher than the 14,000-foot peaks of Colorado.

After a day of getting oriented in the city and enjoying the local market, they met up with Joshua and Gabriela, friends of William and well-known local "Alpinistas" who would be joining them for the expedition. On their first night together, the four of them talked plans and logistics. "Most important, let's clarify our goals for this expedition," William prompted, which made Ben think, *this goal-setting stuff doesn't just apply to the workplace.* Ben could see now why it was critical that everyone be on the same page, especially given the different skill levels among the four climbers, and the language and cultural barriers that could affect their communication on the mountain. By the time the conversation was over, Ben realized that William had just "aligned the team," and without a whiteboard.

The first week of the trip was dedicated to readying their bodies for the diminished oxygen on the big peaks by slowly trekking and living at higher altitudes. They climbed the nontechnical Ruccu Pinchincha that peered over Quito at 15,100 feet. They spent one night camping at 13,000 feet and another one sleeping in a mountain hut at 15,500 feet, then climbed Illiniza Norte, a fun, snow-covered peak that tested their endurance on an easy technical route above 16,000 feet. They attempted the nearby Illiniza Sur but had to back off because of deteriorating snowpack conditions and concern about an avalanche. After four nights of living at high altitude, they were ready for a comfortable night back in Quito before moving on to Cayambe.

So far, Ben's experience with his new climbing team reminded him of his early transition to taking over from John as manager. He recalled the confusion over his role and his resultant tendency to micromanage. He didn't want to make the same mistakes on this expedition, so he asked the climbing team to clarify his role and how they would work with four people climbing on one rope.

He also remembered Stephanie's words during their last meeting together, regarding leadership not being about a silver bullet or a complex theory, but about doing the basics on a consistent basis, in which case he would be tremendously successful. He realized he could apply all of the same leadership principles to this expedition, if not to most areas of his life. With his goals clear, Ben asked his team members for feedback; on one occasion, he even gave some to Joshua so they were clear on what commands to use on slopes that required a belay.

Ben also made it a priority to lead by example by being ready on time, volunteering to carry extra gear, and helping with such team logistics as cooking and route planning.

Just as important, he made an immediate effort to get to know Joshua and Gabriela and to build cohesion quickly. Stephanie's voice echoed in his brain: *It's not enough for your team members to be working on the right things. They have to work on the right things...together.* That meant creating transparency among team members, generating a team environment of open communication, and getting to know each other at a deeper level that would build trust. It was BCO-Tek all over again, except at the top of the world.

In William, Ben could clearly see the skills it took to engage and cultivate a team. William regularly recognized people when they contributed to their shared goals. He delegated so as not to come across as being a taskmaster; rather, he included others, gave them new opportunities to develop, and allowed them to tackle higher-level tasks such as finalizing the climbing permits needed on the taller mountains.

Finally, it was evident that everyone on the climbing team was encouraging each other to learn and develop. They debriefed each other after climbing Ruccu Pinchincha, Illiniza Norte, and Illiniza Sur, and thus were able to fine-tune their glacier travel techniques and teamwork. They even came up with a few new ideas for improving safety and efficiency.

With the team acclimated, they were ready for the taller peaks. The four of them packed into Joshua's Toyota truck and headed north toward the agricultural town of Cayambe. Along the way they stopped at the Mitad del Mundo, a monument marking a point in the road that crossed the equator. From there, they'd access a rocky dirt road and take it to a mountain hut that sat at the base of the Cayambe Volcano over 15,000 feet above sea level.

They spent the first night at the hut acclimating, and the following day scouting the route across a rocky and exposed slope they would have to cross at night prior to getting to the foot of the glacier. On summit day they left the hut at 1:30 a.m. and tracked through the night. They stepped up intensity and focus as they encountered large and intimidating crevasses. At increased elevations, the near-whiteout conditions made navigation harder. They punched through to the summit at about 6:30 a.m. after nearly five hours of climbing, spent twenty minutes on top recovering, then began their descent. They were back at the hut by 10:00 a.m. There the team members celebrated their success and conducted a debrief. Ben learned a few more things about glacier travel that could only come with experience. This reinforced the need for continued learning and development as a means to keep safe on the mountain while working efficiently as a team.

They went back to Quito for two days of rest and relaxation and then on to the high mountain hut on Cotopaxi. They settled into bed around seven o'clock on summit night. Even though they were too excited to sleep, it was important to spend a few hours off their feet. Ben was the first to get up at 11:30 p.m., and everyone was out of the hut for their summit attempt an hour later. They'd have about 5,000 feet of elevation gain if they were successful.

Their work and focus from climbs on Illiniza Norte and Cayambe paid off. The team moved well together and communicated effectively. To top it off, the weather was perfect. At sunrise they were on the final fifty-degree headwall, the position of the mountain against the rising sun casting a huge triangular shadow in the distance. One step at a time, foot over foot, they worked until they finally crested the summit at 7:30 a.m.

The views were unending. The team was even able to see into the caldera, the center of the volcano. Ben felt a deep, abiding sense of accomplishment and satisfaction. He had gotten this far because he was part of a team, one that was aligned around common goals and worked cohesively. He had reached a higher level, and he knew it was not just in the mountains, but as a leader as well. Even though his body was tired, he felt refreshed and reenergized as he saw very clearly, for the first time, that leadership was about doing certain things on a consistent basis—leading by example, aligning the team, building cohesion, engaging and cultivating.

And most important: putting his people first.

II The People-First Leadership™ Model

Overview

People-First Leadership™ is both a set of principles that leaders can implement and a philosophy of leading. The principles were outlined in our parable at a high level by Stephanie, the vice president and Ben's boss, and are laid out in much more detail in this section of the book. This philosophy is one that I developed over the span of my career as I noticed that successful organizations put their people first and, as a result, are able to create a sustainable competitive edge.

As you transition into your role as leader, you may be tempted to look for a "silver bullet" to make things easier. I believe that the answers are more practical and that you should focus on your people first by doing the following:

- Lead by Example

- Align Your Team

- Build Cohesion

- Engage and Cultivate

Focus on these four factors and you'll ignite your potential as a leader, along with the potential of the people who report to you.

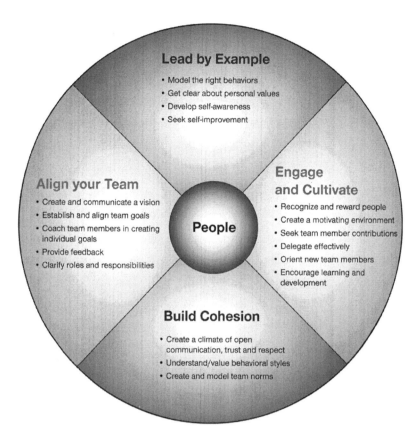

For additional tools and templates on how to best implement each of the four factors, go to our website at http://www.512solutions.com and click on Free Resources.

Let's explore these four factors in greater detail.

People-First Leadership Factor 1: Lead by Example

Have you ever respected any leaders whose words did not match their actions? Have you ever had respect for a leader who preached personal values, yet behaved differently?

The fundamental component of **People-First Leadership**™ is to Lead by Example. This is the core component that will either establish your credibility or kill it. Just remember: *Lack of credibility will prevent you from earning commitment and trust from your team members.* Without that, there is no leadership.

To determine where you are as a person who Leads by Example, ask yourself the following question:

Would you work for you?

Think about it. Would you respect yourself based on the behaviors you exhibit today? Would you find yourself credible? Would you be committed to *you*?

Leading by Example has nothing to do with charisma, or with being a public hero. It is not dictated by the traits you were born with. It is simply about personal alignment.

People-First Leaders™ generate commitment as they Lead by Example by focusing on the following actions:

- **They go first.** Leaders never ask others to do something they wouldn't do themselves.

- **They model the behaviors they want to see in others.** This might mean demonstrating your competency. Or like Ben Turner, coming in on a Saturday morning when you expect others to do likewise. You might even have to show up earlier and stay later, or be first to contribute before asking it of others. There are many ways to lead by example, and thousands of opportunities for it every day.

- **They are clear about their personal values, and act accordingly.** Our values aren't something we check at the door when we step into the workplace. They follow us around and exhibit themselves in subtle ways. They have an impact on our every behavior. When leaders aren't clear about their personal values, they tend to say one thing and act very differently.

- **They know themselves.** Effective leaders understand how their personal style affects the people around them—peers, team members, managers. They understand why they respond to others the way they do. **People-First** leaders have a deep sense of self-awareness and like to explore, challenge, and learn about themselves and their emotions.

- **They seek self-improvement.** There is no one destination in leadership development. Finishing a two-day course or a nine-month program doesn't mean you have arrived. Being an effective and impactful leader requires that you constantly develop and learn, always seeking self-improvement.

Mistakes Leaders Make

There are two common and costly mistakes leaders make that can result in a loss of credibility and trust.

MISTAKE 1: Getting caught up in the Popeye Syndrome—"I am what I am."

The implied message here is: "I am the way I am and if you don't like it, who cares?" We saw Ben exhibit this behavior when he conducted his meetings without involving his team members, and when he resolved Angela's issues without asking for her input or engaging her in the problem-solving process.

The trouble with the Popeye Syndrome is that it's ineffective. It assumes that things don't change and circumstances don't change, and that all individuals need exactly the same things from their leaders. None of this is true. Leading by Example requires leaders to know who they are while being constantly in search of self-improvement. They also must have a keen sense of the individual needs of each team member.

MISTAKE 2: Leading by e-mail (or by texting, project management tools, online chat, or other technology) instead of Leading by Example.

Technology is a lovely thing. It makes your job and your life easier in hundreds of ways. However, it can also be used as a smokescreen to avoid difficult conversations, or to dispatch delicate communications bluntly. Leaders make this mistake when they provide feedback by e-mail, delegate by e-mail, and reset expectations by hitting the Send key...often with the team member sitting in the very next cubicle! In the story you read, this was Darryl's tendency as he found comfort in keeping difficult conversations at a digital distance. You might remember how he provided one of his people with a written warning via e-mail instead of in person, and you probably noticed his overreliance on "collaboration tools" to assign tasks and set expectations.

Leading by Example means being out there as a leader, getting in the mud with your people. It's about being visible and available by walking around each day, showing up at functions, being in the mix. If your team members work remotely, make sure you connect with them by phone every other day, and in person once per quarter. You can't go first or model the behaviors you want to see in others from behind a high-tech computer monitor.

Tips for Making the Transition from Peer to Manager

Making the transition from peer to manager can be challenging. The change of status and responsibility almost always affects both professional and personal relationships. In Ben's story, we saw the pitfalls inherent in two very different leadership styles.

Ben was dominant and overly concerned about losing control. Someone like Ben can Lead by Example by shifting from the behaviors in the left column to those on the right:

Ben's Old Behaviors	People-First Leadership Behaviors
Micromanaging tasks and people	Setting clear expectations, providing necessary support, following up at regular intervals
Communicating aggressively	Communicating assertively by being direct yet professional
Withholding knowledge and relevant information	Being transparent, communicating what is known and not known
Being overly focused on tasks and results	Recognizing and encouraging those who contribute to the results

Meanwhile, Darryl was timid and preoccupied with being accepted. New managers who struggle with similar issues can Lead by Example by shifting from the behaviors in the left column to those on the right:

Darryl's Old Behaviors	People-First Leadership Behaviors
Being vague about what he is requesting	Being assertive by providing direct and specific expectations
Adopting hands-off style for fear of imposing	Providing specific direction and proactively following up
Worrying about what his people will think of him	Focusing on what is right for the team and the business
Avoiding conflict and difficult conversations	Encouraging challenges to ideas, providing timely feedback, demanding excellence

As a new leader, you must understand that you will be called upon to do many things, and that leadership often requires a balance of what can seem like opposing characteristics. To effectively Lead by Example, a leader must balance courage with humility. Courage is defined as boldness or bravery, and when it comes to leadership this means having the boldness or bravery to do the right things—especially when the right things are difficult to do! It takes courage to go first, give people direct feedback, and conduct difficult discussions regarding performance. It takes courage to lead people through change, to deal with conflict head-on (instead of letting it simmer beneath the surface), and to share an opposing viewpoint in a meeting where everyone else is thinking alike.

Stephanie was a courageous leader. She dedicated a large portion of her time to coaching and supporting Ben and Darryl, and to handling difficult conversations with them head-on.

On the flip side, successful leaders must also be humble. Humility is defined as a lack of vanity or self-importance, and in reference to leadership it means setting aside individual ego and agendas to focus on team objectives. It means pushing problem-solving lower in the organization, giving up some control and decision-making, and empowering people to do their jobs. We saw Ben develop the characteristic of humility when he changed his leadership style to be more inclusive in meetings.

The Results: When leaders lead by example, it results in credibility and trust.

Credibility is when your people respect what you say and what you do, even when they disagree with your decision. They have faith in your competence and confidence in your capabilities.

Trust is when your people are able to rely on you. Have confidence in you. Respect your character.

Today, I challenge you to consider the following:

- Are you Leading by Example both personally and professionally?

- What do your actions say?

- What does your lack of action say?

- What do your words indicate?

- Are you asking others to do things you would not do first?

- Are you the first to step onto the field of battle and the last to leave?

For additional tools and templates on how to best implement the Lead by Example factor, go to our website at http://www.512solutions.com and click on Free Resources.

People-First Leadership Factor 1: Lead by Example

- Align your actions with your words.

- Go first. Never ask others to do what you wouldn't do.

- Credibility is the foundation of respect and trust; it is earned when actions are aligned with words.

- Walk around every day. Leading by e-mail is not Leading by Example.

- Get clear on your personal values and align them with team and organizational values.

- Communicate assertively, not aggressively or reluctantly. Balance courage with humility.

People-First Leadership Factor 2: Align Your Team

As a new leader, one of your primary roles is to ensure your team is aligned. This means getting people to work on the right things. When people are focused on the right things, they are more effective. **People-First Leaders™** generate commitment by doing the following to get their teams aligned:

- Creating and communicating a vision for the team;

- Establishing SMART goals for the team;

- Helping team members develop individual performance goals;

- Providing positive and constructive feedback consistently throughout the year;

- Clarifying roles and responsibilities.

Creating and Communicating a Vision for the Team

Numerous leadership books will tell you that having a vision is important. But for many people, the idea alone is difficult to understand, which makes developing a team vision elusive.

Having a vision for your team is critical because it gives members clarity about the team's purpose and where the team is going. That clarity helps in day-to-day decision-making and prioritizing.

As Stephanie told Ben and Darryl, it isn't rocket science. Because most leaders make this more complicated than necessary, here is a simple formula for creating your team vision:

1. **Identify and communicate your team's purpose.** What is it that your team is designed and destined to do?
2. **Communicate where you would like the team to be.** What is the ideal future state of the team?

3. **Describe how you envision the team will get there.** What are the ways in which you expect the team to operate? What concisely describes how the team will be together? What will the culture of the team be like?

Here's a simple example one of my clients uses as a project team leader: *"Our purpose is to deliver this project on time and on budget. By doing so we will help our client be wildly successful in their business and in turn they will be loyal to us and value our services. We will be a cohesive team with people who support each other, are responsive to our clients, and we'll have fun in the process."*

Simple. Compelling. Easy to remember.

Your team vision isn't designed for marketing purposes or to be a pretty poster on the wall that no one cares about. Your vision is to help you as a leader to align your team. A short one- or two-sentence statement that you can vary for team meetings and individual discussions will help energize people, communicate the bigger picture, and keep everyone focused on the right things.

Establishing SMART Goals for the Team

Having a vision and implementing it are two different things. One of your most exciting challenges will be to bring that vision to life, and for that you will need to establish goals for the overall team based on departmental and/or organizational goals. In establishing goals, you'll help align the team as a whole, and help focus its decision-making and prioritizing.

Each of your team goals should be written as one-sentence statements using the SMART format: Specific, Measurable, Actionable, Realistic, and Time-oriented. It is often helpful to break those goals down into more detailed action plans to reduce complexity and create achievable milestones. Additionally, your team goals should be posted in a central location to create transparency, open communication, and accountability, just as Stephanie did when she posted them on her office window.

Helping Team Members Develop Individual Performance Goals

After team goals have been established, link your vision for the team with members' personal aspirations by asking each of them to create individual performance goals. Similar to team goals, these should follow the SMART format.

It is imperative that they be established in a collaborative manner where the team member is actively involved in the goal-setting process. To do this, share the team goals with everyone and give them time to craft their individual performance goals. Follow up with a two-way private conversation, and coach and negotiate until their individual performance goals meet your expectations. In our story, Ben did more coaching and negotiation with Jen and Angela, his less-experienced team members, than with the more experienced Kevin.

To keep the goal-setting process personal and inspiring, ask each person to tell you about where they want to be in their careers and what type of environment is motivating to them. That gives you great information on how to develop, delegate, direct, and recognize your people. Once Ben had gotten feedback on team members' individual aspirations, he was able to successfully link his recognition efforts to those particular aspirations. This gave him insight into the type of environment that was motivating to his people (more on this in **People-First Factor 4: Engage and Cultivate**).

After goals have been agreed to, ask your team member to create an action plan for each, breaking it down into more manageable components with key action items and target completion dates.

At this point, all professional goals should be aligned with team and departmental goals. Additionally, personal goals should support professional development and growth and get people excited about working for you and for the organization, even when there aren't any immediate promotion opportunities. Remember that by involving your team members in the process you build commitment to their goals, to you, and to the organization.

In many companies, strategic goals and objectives at the enterprise level are about as clear as mud. You'll know this is the case if your priorities are constantly in flux. As a new leader, you may find it nearly impossible to influence upper management to clarify higher-level goals. If you discover yourself in this situation, do your best to establish team goals, keep them visible, align individual performance goals with your team goals, and be prepared to make changes along the way as organizational priorities change.

The goal-setting process is one of the most important things you can make happen as a leader. Goals are expectations, and the fact of the matter is that your team members want to know what is expected of them. In the absence of clear expectations they will make up their own, and I guarantee they're not going to be in line with what you expect in your capacity as leader.

Providing Positive and Constructive Feedback Consistently throughout the Year

Giving feedback is often one of the hardest things for people to do in the workplace. It's also one of the most important in terms of leadership. I have seen countless leaders and team members struggle with it—both giving and receiving feedback. Perhaps it is human nature to want to avoid difficult conversations, but when we avoid giving feedback, we are doing a disservice to the team member, the team itself, and the organization as a whole. Such avoidance robs the team member of the opportunity to improve, and causes you to lose credibility as a leader with others on the team, often without even realizing it. Worse, when leaders don't provide feedback on the small things, they are often forced to make bigger decisions—like removing someone from a project or even firing them.

At first, Ben and Darryl avoided providing clear and direct feedback. As a result, they both leaped to the discipline conversation, something much bigger than a feedback discussion. In Ben's case, it led to Angela completely disengaging and then taking her contributions to another organization where she hoped she would matter.

I have found that people generally want feedback, even crave it. They want to know what they are doing well and where they can improve. When feedback is provided in the spirit of helping people elevate their performance, it is much more likely to be accepted in a positive way.

Feedback is the glue that holds alignment together. Regardless of format, feedback should encompass the following characteristics:

- **It should be delivered in a timely fashion** so a team member can correlate a specific behavior with what went well or what needs to change.

- **It should be specific and behavior-based** to give people clarity about what to keep doing and what to change.

- **It should be owned by the leader.** If you find yourself sharing feedback with a team member and prefacing it with "we," you are likely hiding behind the cover of others instead of taking ownership of it.

Here is a simple framework you can use to ensure you are providing feedback on a consistent basis:

The *A-ha!* Moment

The *A-ha!* moment is the random, unscheduled opportunity for you to provide both positive and constructive feedback. When you observe a behavior you want to see repeated, give positive feedback. When it's a behavior you *don't* want to see repeated, give constructive feedback.

A simple way to provide constructive feedback is to use the Situation-Impact-Input-Follow-up format that Stephanie outlined in the parable:

- **Situation:** Begin by describing the behavior you saw as specifically as possible. Most people follow a general rule of providing constructive feedback in private and positive feedback in public, but be careful: Some people prefer not to receive praise in public, so get to know your team members and their individual preferences, although there may be times when it is necessary to provide constructive feedback in a public forum.

- **Impact:** Next, describe the impact of the behavior—on you, other team members, your customers, etc. Describing the impact will help team members understand the consequences of their behavior.

- **Input:** Third, ask for input from team members on what they can do to improve. Actively participating in coming up with solutions means they will be much more committed to the solution.

- **Follow-up:** Fourth, schedule time for follow-up. This is the most commonly overlooked step in providing feedback, at the risk of derailing the entire enterprise. Follow-up reinforces behavioral change and increases the likelihood of improving performance.

When done right, the process of providing feedback should maintain or build a team member's self-esteem while helping improve performance. By doing that, you also build productivity, job satisfaction, and commitment.

Monthly One-on-One Meetings

Just as Stephanie did with Ben and Darryl, all leaders should conduct one-on-ones with each of their direct reports at least once a month. This is an opportunity to open the lines of communication, understand what they need from you to be most effective, and provide support and feedback. Keep the sessions informal and have your team member establish the agenda ahead of time. Finally, make sure these are *scheduled appointments*. What gets scheduled gets done. What doesn't, gets postponed...indefinitely.

Quarterly Goal Reviews

In most organizations, goals are created at the beginning of the performance year and then buried in a dark place, never to be found again. This is the primary reason actions are rarely aligned and the performance management system breaks down. This is your opportunity to shine as a leader and make a significant impact on your people and your organization.

At least once a quarter, replace one of your regularly scheduled one-on-ones with a slightly more formal goal review. In addition to the usual topics, review your team member's performance goals, ask for input on performance relative to those goals, provide both positive and constructive input, make adjustments to the goals as needed, and agree on a date to review any plans for improvement or support needed.

Annual Performance Review

If feedback is provided regularly throughout the year during *A-ha!* moments, all the rest—monthly one-on-ones, quarterly goal reviews, the annual review—should simply be a summary of a team member's performance. Let me state that more directly: DO NOT SURPRISE EMPLOYEES AT ANNUAL REVIEWS WITH FEEDBACK THEY NEVER RECEIVED DURING THE PERFORMANCE YEAR! There are no exceptions to this rule. Remember what happened to Angela.

To get the most out of the annual review process, ask team members to document their annual performance and e-mail it to you prior to the session. This will give you an opportunity to involve them in the process and also see how well your feedback is aligned with their perception of how they're doing. During the session itself, establish a tone of open communication to build trust, dissolve defensiveness and anxiety, and engender a more productive conversation. Continue that conversation by asking how they thought they performed. Provide your feedback. For development areas, ask them to generate ideas on how they can improve, and agree on a time to review progress during a monthly one-on-one or at another scheduled time.

Finally, to make the whole process easier for you, keep a log through-out the year for each team member. Chart what they did well and what improvement opportunities exist. This will help you avoid the bias of providing feedback only on recent performance or on what has stood out to you lately.

Providing performance feedback requires courage and is critical to everyone's success. When you take the time to do it on small things along the way, you have more options. The other way, you'll wind up with situations where removing someone from a project team or the organization is the only option left.

What Happens When Feedback Doesn't Work?

Oftentimes, feedback does not result in the desired behavioral change, and you must have the courage to quickly move into a discipline process. Allowing poor performance to linger just costs too much—to the organization, to other team members, and to your credibility as a leader.

Most organizations have a discipline policy to follow that escalates with each step. Follow that policy while keeping these key concepts in mind:

- Discipline, like feedback, is designed to help a team member improve performance.

- Conduct your discipline discussions in a way that does not embarrass or undermine the person.

- Provide clear documentation on what was discussed and the performance improvement action steps required.

- Rigorously follow up to ensure that behavioral change happens.

If a team member does not change behavior as a result of the discipline process, the leader must take action to either find a role that is a better fit, or move the person out of the organization.

Clarifying Roles and Responsibilities

It's a bit like the 400-meter relay. Passing the baton is typically done blind. The outgoing runner does not look back. It is the responsibility of the incoming runner to thrust the baton into the outstretched hand and not let go until the outgoing runner takes hold.

In the workplace, too often the baton is dropped because there are gaps in what people think they should be doing and what others think those people should be doing. Close the gaps by clarifying:

a. key task responsibility,

b. decision-making authority, and

c. expectations between teams and departments.

Mistakes Leaders Make

Here are some common and costly mistakes leaders often make that result in a lack of focus and commitment:

MISTAKE 1: Surprising an employee with discipline before providing formal feedback.

We saw the situation in our story when Ben gave Angela a written warning (and made her sign the document on the spot!) without providing her with clear feedback first. Within minutes of that meeting's conclusion, Angela was completely disengaged from her job. A few weeks later, she jumped ship to another organization. This happens in real life all too often in the workplace, and with similar results: A good employee quits. Feedback should be clear prior to starting any discipline process, although there are exceptions, as when team members do something egregious, like engage in harassment or theft. In general, though, surprising an employee with discipline is typically the symptom of a manager who is reluctant to engage in difficult discussions, and not so much about an employee doing anything wrong.

MISTAKE 2: Delaying performance expectations.

Often, team members don't receive their performance goals until one or two months into the performance year, or even later. Delaying performance expectations is typically a symptom of a broken process within the organization or the reluctance of a leader to establish high expectations. Ben and Darryl both waited until Stephanie emphasized the importance of getting expectations into place. Performance goals should be established by the first day of the performance year, which means starting the process early.

MISTAKE 3: Imposing goals on team members.

I can't stress enough the importance of making the goal-setting process collaborative. Imposing individual goals on someone is the fastest way to lose commitment. In Darryl's case, he tried to impose expectations through his online collaboration tool. Technology can be successfully used to support the goal-setting process, but should never take the place of crucial conversations. It is imperative to involve your people in the process and provide coaching along the way to ensure they meet your high expectations.

MISTAKE 4: Smothering feedback with positives on the front and back end.

Don't get me wrong; I'm not asking you to be ruthless! The challenge for most people is that they don't want to hurt anyone's feelings, and in the process they provide feedback that is so fluffy they never state the main point. This results in a message without any clarity. If you plan to sandwich your feedback with positives, make sure the constructive part of the feedback is clear.

MISTAKE 5: Using a one-size-fits-all approach.

Each of your people will come to the team with different levels of maturity, experience, and strength. It is important to adjust how much time and coaching you spend with them based on individual needs. In our story, Jen required somewhat more coaching because of her relative lack of experience, while Kevin needed less.

Tips for the New Manager

Often, new managers make the transition into management after having had a personal relationship with the people they now lead. As a manager, you are expected to produce results and hold people accountable for their contribution to those results, and it's hard to do that with people you used to pal around with over burgers 'n' brew.

This is exactly why establishing performance expectations early is critical to your success and credibility. If you have a personal relationship with the people who are now your direct reports, have a conversation that includes the following topics:

- areas that will be different in your relationship;

- areas that will be similar;

- expectations you have of them as their leader;

- expectations they have of you as their leader.

You will also have to work with your manager to clarify how your new role as a leader will change things for you. Continuing to do everything you did before, while layering on leadership and management responsibilities, is setting yourself up for failure. Being on the same page with your manager as soon as possible will be critical to your success. Two key questions I recommend you and your manager discuss are:

- What will you *stop* doing now that you are in a management position?

- What will you *start* doing now that you are in a management position?

New managers who are reluctant out of a need for acceptance may be tempted to take a hands-off approach to establishing performance expectations. You might even hear yourself saying, "I just want to empower my people and let them do it themselves." However, as we saw with Darryl in our parable, an overly hands-off approach can leave your people frustrated by the lack of direction.

If you're a new manager whose reluctance stems from a fear of losing control, your tendency might be to overmanage or micromanage. You might even hear yourself saying, "It's faster to do this myself than to give it to others." This can be frustrating for team members who value independence and autonomy, and can be misconstrued as not valuing their contributions. Focus on actively listening and asking good questions.

To keep your team aligned effectively, you have to balance two additional and opposing characteristics. On one hand, you must be demanding. On the other, empathetic.

"Demanding" means requiring or claiming more than is generally thought to be fair. In terms of leadership, it means having high expectations, focusing on results, and expecting the best from your people—even in the face of change. In general, people live up to the expectations that are set for them, so when expectations are low, performance is low. When high, performance is high. Being demanding also means holding people accountable to agreed-upon standards, goals, and values.

On the flip side, leaders also have to be empathetic. According to the dictionary, empathy means *being able to identify with the feelings, thoughts, or attitudes of others.* In terms of leadership, empathy is the ability to stand in another person's shoes—to really get the unique challenges, strengths, and talents an individual brings to the team, and to take those challenges, strengths, and talents and create an environment that is motivating to each person. Being empathetic is a key component in building trust.

Making the shift from peer to manager is not easy, but by quickly aligning your individual actions as a leader and the actions and behaviors of your people, the transition will be meaningful and well received.

The Results: With alignment comes clarity and accountability.

With clarity, people understand whom they report to and what they must do, but the idea goes far beyond that. In the Army, leaders communicate the big picture of a mission in the "Commander's Intent" section of an operations order. This enables soldiers to make decisions and take action even when situations are ambiguous. In the workplace, clarity also means understanding how you fit into the overall organizational mission while retaining the freedom to do what needs to be done to accomplish the goal.

By accountability, I mean taking clear responsibility for a plan, process, task, or procedure, and following through to its completion.

Today, I challenge you to consider the following:

• Have you created and communicated a vision for the team?

- Are team goals clear?

- Are individual performance goals (expectations) clear?

- Are you providing feedback on a regular basis through A-ha! moments, monthly one-on-ones, quarterly goal reviews, and the annual review process?

- Do you have the courage to discipline team members if behavioral change doesn't happen after consistent and clear feedback is provided?

For additional tools and templates on how to best implement the Align Your Team factor, go to our website at http://www.512solutions.com and click on Free Resources.

People-First Leadership Factor 2: Align Your Team

- Create and communicate a vision for your team (don't overcomplicate!).

- Establish performance expectations early.

- Don't avoid the difficult conversations. Provide feedback on a consistent basis through *A-ha!* moments, monthly one-on-ones, quarterly goal reviews, and the annual review process.

- When feedback doesn't work, shift to a discipline process—but remember that both feedback and discipline are intended to help a team member improve performance.

- Clarify roles and responsibilities to facilitate handoffs between individuals and teams.

- Respect others' self-esteem in all you do.

- Balance being demanding with empathy.

People-First Leadership Factor 3: Build Cohesion

If the standard in today's workplace is to do more with less, then people have to be able to do more with less...*together.* Easier said than done, as we all bring our different perspectives, goals, values, and backgrounds into the workplace. We have different ways of seeing the world and different preferences for how we approach our work. Those differences don't make it easier to get along or solve problems, but when leaders seek people who think exactly the way they do and have the same exact needs, their teams tend to attract the three unwelcome cousins—groupthink, mediocrity, and stagnation.

People-First Leaders™ build cohesion by creating a culture that knows how to value and leverage the differences people bring into the workplace. General George S. Patton said it best: "If everyone is thinking alike, no one is thinking at all."

Personal differences create differences of opinion, and that's good! When those differences are understood and valued, the outcomes tend to be richer and more innovative. In order to value differences, the culture must be founded on respect and trust. Without respect you can't have trust, and without trust, it's impossible to work on the right things together. Respect and trust become the cornerstones of efficiency and cohesion.

Let's explore in more detail how **People-First Leaders™** generate commitment by building cohesion.

Create a climate of open communication.

Establishing an environment of open communication allows people to share differences of opinion and ideas. It's an environment where leaders involve their people in solving problems, establishing goals, making decisions, and debating ideas so that new ones can emerge. It's also a setting in which leaders share what they know and admit what they don't. Ben began to create an environment of open communication when he changed his meeting format to emphasize input from his team members. Stephanie created an open environment of communication through her monthly town hall meetings and by posting team results on her office window.

Understand and value style differences.

In many of my team and leadership development programs we use a personality style profile tool called DiSC© to help people understand themselves and others at a much deeper level. DiSC© (notice the lowercase "i" to distinguish it from knockoffs), published by Inscape Publishing, provides a practical and effective framework people can use on an interactive basis to improve communication and build cohesion. Additionally, when leaders and team members share their DiSC© styles with each other it helps to build what author Patrick Lencioni calls "vulnerability-based trust," in which team members "comfortably and quickly acknowledge without provocation their mistakes, weaknesses, failures, and needs for help," along with recognizing "the strengths of others, even when those strengths exceed their own."

From a leadership perspective, understanding the ins and outs of behavioral styles helps leaders recognize that a one-size-fits-all approach to communication isn't effective. Using DiSC© effectively can help leaders tailor how they direct, develop, motivate, and delegate to their people and communicate up to their managers.

Another tool that helps leaders understand their own behavioral style is the 363 for Leaders Profile, also published by Inscape Publishing. The profile gathers 360-degree feedback from a leader's direct reports, as well as peers, managers, and others to help leaders understand how they are perceived by the people they work with on a regular basis.

Using both of these profiles helps **People-First Leaders™** develop the self-awareness that is critical to their success. They learn to recognize how their leadership style affects others, and to better understand why they respond to others the way they do.

Clarify, communicate, and model team values.

People-First Leaders™ help create a foundation of trust by establishing a common set of shared values and then appealing to the individual values of others. When we talked about alignment in **People-First Leadership Factor 2**, we focused on mission or task alignment. Creating and modeling values takes alignment beyond just task orientation to a whole new level of behavior. Values guide our behaviors, and behaviors are what make people effective. You can't enact enough laws, policies, and standard operating procedures to govern human behaviors. There has to be something higher-level providing clarity around values.

Create and model team norms.

Norms will take hold on a team regardless of whether they are written down. When they aren't intentionally created, ineffective norms sneak in, such as the way everyone on Ben's team arrived four to seven minutes late for meetings at the beginning of the learning parable. Team norms establish specific guideposts to help a team be most effective. They outline what team time looks like, how decisions are made and meetings conducted, how conflict is handled, and more. The best leaders keep those norms visible and review them prior to regularly scheduled meetings. Also, and most important, they hold themselves and their team members accountable to the established norms.

Understand what people need from each other and what frustrates them.

This is a simple exercise any leader can run. Starting with yourself, communicate what you need from others to be successful, along with what frustrates you. Allow time for this exercise and encourage people to take notes. This is a great opportunity to build trust, understand each other more deeply, and create an environment of open communication. When Ben and Darryl conducted this exercise with their teams, everyone learned more about what made each other tick.

Mistakes Leaders Make

Here are some common and costly mistakes leaders make that result in a loss of trust and cohesion:

MISTAKE 1: Getting stuck in always having to be right.

This mistake is dangerous because it ultimately squelches creativity and innovation. You probably remember the scene where Ben disregarded Henry's input during a team meeting. Behavior like this limits constructive conflict and debate, and devalues others' opinions. When leaders shoot down ideas that don't mesh with their own, their team members will be less likely to contribute in the future. This breakdown is common with leaders who have not yet established a strong foundation of trust and open communication. It's also a sign of leaders who have a weak sense of self-awareness or an inflated ego.

MISTAKE 2: Solving problems others should solve.

It's not uncommon for new leaders to solve problems for their team members instead of helping them learn to do it on their own. If you're an overly controlling leader, you may find it faster to take care of it yourself than to take the time to teach. We saw Ben "save the day" when Angela was struggling, although this actually left her feeling more confused and helpless. For the less assertive leader, it might be easier to do it yourself so you can get around confronting an issue directly. When you solve problems for your team members, they don't get the chance to grow and stretch, and you limit their future effectiveness. By doing it for them, you're not holding people accountable for their own work, and this actually deflates trust and commitment. It also bogs you down in being the "doer" instead of focusing on higher-level issues and managing your team. Part of your role as a new leader is to coach, support, and teach the people you now lead.

MISTAKE 3: Leading with answers instead of questions.

Jim Collins said it best in *Good to Great*: Leading from good to great does not mean coming up with the answers and then motivating everyone to follow your messianic vision. It means having the humility to grasp that you do not yet understand enough to have all the answers, and to ask the questions that will lead to the best possible insights. Once you grasp this concept as a new manager, you will quickly make strides toward building a culture of trust and respect. Leading with questions instead of answers opens conversation and shows your people you value their input.

MISTAKE 4: Making decisions by consensus.

Consensus is a good decision-making method for summer picnics and bowling outings. It's deadly for a team like yours.

In most cases, teams do not truly understand what consensus means. Even when they do, that typically results in an "illusion of consensus," where a few loud people speak for the group even if they do not represent everyone's opinion. Trying to appease everyone through consensus results in slow decision-making and missed opportunities.

That said, there is a critical element of the consensus process that's important—ensuring that everyone's voice is heard. When people have the opportunity to speak, they feel their contributions matter, and thereby become more committed to leader and organization alike, even when they disagree with the final decision. Instead of wasting time trying to make decisions by consensus, focus on getting everyone to participate, listening to each other's ideas, and engaging in constructive debate.

MISTAKE 5: Asking for input after a decision has been made.

People can see right through this mistake. If you have already made a decision and are set on a course of action, asking for opinions after the fact merely because you think it will appease others will backfire. If you aren't really interested in hearing any input, don't ask for it. Certainly don't paper it over with an artificial, insincere inquiry.

Tips for the New Manager

For new leaders who tend to be reluctant because they fear not finding acceptance, implementing **People-First Leadership Factor 3: Build Cohesion** will fit with your natural tendency to involve others. Just make sure you assert yourself in the process of actively engaging in debate and sharing your opinion. Your greatest challenge may be making a decision when others don't agree with you. Keep in mind that leadership isn't a popularity contest. Find your voice, and use it.

For new leaders who tend to be reluctant because they fear of loss of control, the challenge in implementing **People-First Leadership Factor 3** is giving up enough control to allow people to participate. It means making an extra effort to ask questions and listen to the answers. Listening sounds simple, but it's not. It is an essential communications tool. Most people think they listen well, but they usually spend more time planning their rebuttal than truly trying to hear and understand. The most influential people in the world are also the best listeners. They're the ones who ask questions, show interest, and speak half as much as you.

Making the transition into leadership requires that you effectively balance two additional opposing characteristics: being driven and staying vulnerable. Having drive means to carry on or through energetically. From a leadership perspective, being driven means becoming focused on business results and having the resolve to do what's right for the organization, such as eliminating poor performers or discontinuing underperforming product lines.

At the same time, a leader must balance that drive with vulnerability. The word means *capable of or susceptible to being wounded or hurt.* From a leadership perspective it means being open to asking others for help, admitting mistakes, and creating a culture where everyone else on your team can do the same.

The Results: When leaders build cohesion, it results in teamwork and efficiency.

By teamwork I mean a focus on team objectives instead of individual goals and agendas. It's a commitment to a common and shared purpose.

By efficiency I mean finding ways to be faster and better by challenging others' ideas, committing to decisions, and moving forward as a team.

Today, I challenge you to consider the following:

- Are you building cohesion?

- Have you created an open environment of communication by involving team members in problem-solving, debate, and decision-making?

- Do you and your people understand and value differences?

- Are values stated and clear?

- Do team norms guide behaviors?

- Do all members of your team understand what they need from each other and what frustrates them?

- Are you leading with questions instead of answers?

For additional tools and templates on how to best implement the Build Cohesion factor, go to our website at http://www.512solutions.com and click on Free Resources.

People-First Leadership Factor 3: Build Cohesion
- Create an environment based on respect and trust, the cornerstones of efficiency.
- Enable open communication and encourage dialogue and debate.
- Value differences.
- Understand behavioral styles.
- Clarify and model team values.
- Create and implement team norms, and hold yourself and others accountable to them.
- Understand what people need and what frustrates them.
- Balance drive with vulnerability.

People-First Leadership Factor 4: Engage and Cultivate

Ask soldiers why they would risk their life to save one of their own and they will tell you it's about commitment—commitment to their fellow soldiers. This was one of the primary reasons Stephanie suggested that Ben and Darryl see *We Were Soldiers*. In that movie the primary leader, Lieutenant Colonel Moore, continually focused on building commitment among his leaders and soldiers.

People-First Leadership Factor 4 is about building employee commitment by engaging team members at an individual level and cultivating them as people and employees. As a leader, you have the greatest impact on team member commitment and engagement, and in most cases, as Stephanie told Ben and Darryl in our story, people leave their managers, not their organizations.

You can't build commitment through policies. You can't create it through standard operating procedures. You can't demand it through directives. Commitment arises from relationships. It is derived from being able to relate to people as individuals.

Clearly, a one-size-fits-all approach is not going to work. People respond to you based on how they are treated. If you affect people positively, you'll build commitment; affect them negatively and you'll only gain compliance, where they do just enough to get by. What type of team would you rather build—one that is compliant or committed?

People-First Leaders™ build commitment by engaging and cultivating their people in the following ways:

- recognizing and rewarding their people;

- creating a motivating environment for each team member;

- seeking and valuing team member contributions;

- delegating effectively;

- orienting new team members;

- encouraging learning and development.

Let's look at each of these individually.

Recognize and reward your people.

Recognition is a core component of building team member commitment. It shows people that their contributions matter and that they are valued members of a team. In fact, Donald Clifton writes in his book *How Full Is Your Bucket?* that the primary reason people leave their jobs is they don't feel appreciated. I have seen countless examples of people leaving jobs in search of more rewarding opportunities.

Here are three building blocks for making your recognition efforts work at the team level. These building blocks were inspired by the book *The Carrot Principle* by Adrian Gostick and Chester Elton.

Building Block 1: *A-ha!* Moments

Similar to the way we defined feedback in **People-First Factor 2**, A-ha! moments are random, unscheduled opportunities to provide recognition to your team members. When you observe a behavior you want to see repeated, provide recognition. Make sure it's specific, communicates the impact of your team member's behavior, and is frequent and timely.

Building Block 2: Above-and-Beyond Recognition

Above-and-beyond recognition takes it to another level when people make a significant contribution to the organization, its bottom line, or its customers. Ben created a program to reward team members who went above and beyond by tailoring his recognition efforts to what his people needed and wanted. For example, he discovered that Jen was learning Spanish and wanted to travel abroad. Knowing this enabled him to link her personal aspirations to organizational success, so that when Jen accomplished something above and beyond, Ben could recognize her with Visa points she could use toward language lessons. Linking personal aspirations to organizational success (in terms of culture, values, and goals) is incredibly powerful.

Also keep in mind that people prefer to be recognized in different ways. Some enjoy public recognition while others hate the limelight. Some want to be rewarded with time off; others want more challenging projects. There are hundreds of ways to recognize and reward people, and many of them cost little or nothing.

Your challenge as a leader is to recognize people in ways that inspire action and commitment. When people go above and beyond, link their efforts to the goals, values, and culture of the team.

Building Block 3: Team Recognition

Team Recognition, as the name implies, happens when you give a tip of the hat to the entire team for an accomplishment such as completing a project, or for reaching a milestone in the team's history. Taking time to recognize the team as a whole builds loyalty and commitment. Recognition could take the form of a simple announcement at a town hall meeting or a special celebration with the entire team. Make the presentation personal, and take the time to celebrate.

Create a motivating environment for each individual team member.

I firmly believe that you cannot motivate people. *People have to motivate themselves.* That said, **People-First Leaders™** know how to create an environment that is engaging for all by tailoring it to individual needs and preferences. They adapt how they direct, delegate, and develop their team members. They understand how people best receive and process information, and how to make them successful in meetings. Monthly one-on-ones provide a great outlet for many of these things and will help you truly understand what your people need to be successful in the workplace.

How do you know what type of environment is motivating for them? Just ask! Here are a few questions you can use in your next one-on-ones to get started:

- Which three aspects of your work did you like most during the past year?

- What do you like least about your job?

- What are your top three strengths and opportunities for improvement?

- What is something new you would like to try in the coming year?

- What kind of work environment is motivating to you? What gives you energy?

- What are you passionate about?

- What talents and skills do you have that can help this team succeed?

- What do you need from me to be your best?

Seek and value team member contributions.

Involving people in problem-solving and decision-making reinforces that you value people's contributions. When people are involved they are more committed, even to decisions with which they disagree.

A good place to involve people is in meetings. Instead of wasting time updating each other on information that can be shared through e-mail, internal websites, and status reports, solve problems together. The more they get involved, the more engaged they'll be. Ben did this by rotating facilitators at his weekly team meetings, giving people ownership of the outcomes those meetings created.

Delegate effectively.

Delegation does three very important things to help engage and cultivate your people:

1. It demonstrates that you trust them, which in turn helps build their trust in you.
2. It gives your people an opportunity to develop new skills.
3. It frees you up to focus on bigger-picture things that you need to address as a leader, such as thinking about team and departmental objectives, dealing with higher-end customer issues, and planning.

Delegation isn't easy, and you may even hear yourself saying, "It's quicker to just do it myself." That may be true, but the longer you do it yourself, the longer your people won't be developing the skills to do it themselves. Here are a few ideas for making delegation more effective:

1. **Communicate your intent up-front.** Remember the "Commander's Intent" in Army operations orders (see **People-First Leadership Factor 2: Alignment**)? The same can be applied to delegation. Make sure your people understand the overall purpose of the task you are delegating.

2. **Adjust how you delegate based on experience level.** In our story, Kevin was experienced and Ben could delegate simply by providing him high-level objectives. Angela and Jennifer were less experienced, which required Ben to provide more details and support.

3. **Communicate the level of decision-making and authority a team member has relative to the task.** Use this simple Level 1–3 system:

   - Level 1 authority means you want the team member to complete the task, but you will make any decisions necessary.

   - Level 2 authority means you want your team member to complete the task and make recommendations regarding any decisions to be made. You retain the ultimate decision-making authority.

   - Level 3 authority means that your team member has complete responsibility for task completion and decision-making. You just want to stay informed.

4. Check in to ensure understanding and completion. Just because you delegate doesn't mean you give up overall responsibility. Adjust how often you check in with team members based on their level of competence and your level of confidence in them.

Orient new members.

Formally orienting a new person on your team can accelerate the individual's effectiveness and productivity. Do not take this for granted, even though most teams ignore it. In many organizations, Human

Resources goes through an "on-boarding" process that does very little to acclimate a team member to the actual team a new employee will be joining. Here are a few ideas to effectively orient new team members:

- Make a professional first impression by welcoming newcomers and offering to help them through the administrative process. Don't just leave this up to Human Resources! Take them to breakfast or lunch their first day and make informal introductions to their co-workers. This will help them feel connected and welcome.

- At your first team meeting together, review team norms, share DiSC© styles, discuss what each person needs from the others to be successful, and clarify roles and responsibilities. This may take an hour or more for a new team member, but you will save countless hours down the road in improved productivity and reduced conflict.

- Create opportunities for on-the-job training and cross training. No matter what their background and experience level are, new team members need assistance from tenured employees to get on board with policies, procedures, processes, and unwritten expectations and norms.

- Introduce new team members to key players in other departments. Help them understand what other stakeholders expect from the team and who the key influencers are in the organization.

- Check in with new team members on a regular basis (not through e-mail, but in person!) and create an open climate of communication where they feel comfortable coming to you for assistance.

Most turnovers in organizations happen within the first eighteen months of a team member's tenure. You can help reduce this by ensuring that new team members are intentionally oriented to the way things get done and to the team's culture.

Encourage learning and development.

This is ultimately about investment. **People-First Leaders™** invest in their people by providing them with a variety of opportunities to learn and grow on a consistent and ongoing basis. Learning and develop-ment happen through on-the-job training, formal or informal mentoring, monthly one-on-one coaching, lunch-and-learn sessions, formal training and development programs, monthly town hall meetings, online learning, webinars, and other creative approaches.

Investing in people first is the only way to ensure a competitive edge well beyond quarterly earnings. Learning crushes complacency. It empowers people to think differently. It nurtures innovation. But it has to be ingrained in the team culture.

Mistakes Leaders Make

Here are three common and costly mistakes leaders make that result in low team member engagement and lack of commitment:

MISTAKE 1: Focusing on what *you* need instead of what your people need.

I often hear leaders complaining, "Why should I recognize people for doing their jobs? This is what they get paid to do." Or, "I don't need daily inspiration, neither should my people." Or, "You should know you're doing a good job because you got a pay raise this year."

What is true for you as an individual is not necessarily true for others. Focus on what your team members need and they'll be more committed to you. One of the most important things team members need is to know that their contributions matter.

MISTAKE 2: Drawing clear lines in the sand.

The challenge in many organizations is that most leaders don't get to know their people well enough to create a motivating environment. They like to draw lines in the sand between business and personal. Actually, our business and personal lives often intersect and have a huge impact on each other.

We need to make business *personal*. The more you know your people on a personal and individual level, the better you can lead them.

MISTAKE 3: Providing recognition through general praise.

Using general recognition statements like "You're doing a great job" or "Keep up the good work" doesn't make a positive impact on anyone. It can actually create resentment by sending an obvious signal that you have no idea what they are doing or working on. Make sure your recognition is specific and timely. If people have gone above and beyond, communicate how their contributions have had a positive impact on team goals and values.

Tips for the New Manager

If you're a new leader who tends to be reluctant because you fear not finding acceptance, take the initiative to provide more support and structure to your people. Make sure you are visible and available—not just through technology, but also in person.

If you're a new leader who tends to be reluctant because you fear loss of control, spend more time seeking input, listening, delegating, and asking questions. Give your people the leeway to fail forward—the opportunity to make mistakes and learn from them.

Making the transition into leadership requires that you effectively balance two additional and opposing characteristics: consistency and curiosity. Consistency, on one hand, means steadfast adherence to the same principles, course, or form. In terms of leadership, consistency means providing stability during turbulent times, being steadfast in purpose and vision in the face of resistance, and being intentional about how you engage and cultivate your team. Curiosity, on the other hand, helps balance the steadiness required of leaders. Curiosity means *an intense desire to know and understand.* Like a child, a leader has to be eager to grow and have the inquisitiveness to find out more. Curiosity is about expanding knowledge, having the agility to change, and learning more about industry, business, team members—and, most important, *self.*

The Results: When leaders engage and cultivate team members, it results in dedication and innovation.

By dedication, I mean people taking ownership of their work and following through to make sure the customer, team members, and organization are served. When people are at work, they are productive and focused on doing things well for the betterment of themselves, their team, and the organization.

By innovation, I mean team members acting like entrepreneurs and proactively responding to changing market conditions, customer needs, and internal team processes.

Today, I challenge you to consider the following:

- Do you recognize people during *A-ha!* moments, for above-and-beyond efforts, and at the team level?

- Do you know what is motivating to each of your individual team members?

- Are you orienting new team members?

- Are you seeking input from your team members and delegating effectively?

- Do you encourage learning and development?

For additional tools and templates on how to best implement the Engage and Cultivate factor, go to our website at http://www.512solutions.com and click on Free Resources.

People-First Leadership Factor 4: Engage and Cultivate
• Tailor your recognition efforts to the individual. • Understand what people need. What motivates them? • Value the contributions of your team members. • Delegate to build competence, reinforce trust, and free you for bigger-picture initiatives. • Orient new team members to accelerate their integration into the team. • Invest in your people through formal and informal learning and development opportunities. • Balance consistency with curiosity.

Coaching Methods for Senior Leaders

Stephanie's coaching methods are a model for all senior leaders. She understood that she needed to dedicate twenty percent or more of her time coaching her emerging leaders to help shape their development. It's a responsibility that senior leaders all too often overlook as they get caught up in pressing matters, but nothing can be more important to the health and future of an organization.

Coaching emerging leaders not only helps develop their skills, it frees senior leaders to focus on more strategic initiatives as their junior leaders develop. It also builds the bench strength of an organization to ensure a competitive advantage in years to come. To coach your people effectively, emulate Stephanie by doing the following:

Conduct regular one-on-one meetings.

These are critical to creating positive behavioral change. They open the lines of communication and provide an informal yet structured approach to establishing expectations and providing feedback. Make sure these meetings don't turn into project updates! They are intended primarily for emerging-leader development. The time frame between meetings depends largely on the leadership maturity of the emerging leader. At a minimum, senior leaders should meet with their emerging leaders monthly, but they may initially need to provide support on a weekly or even daily basis.

Question, listen, advise, and follow up.

Stephanie's general coaching approach was to advise only after first questioning and listening. This not only helped build buy-in, as her people were truly engaged in the process, but helped her judge how far along they were in their development. Follow-up is the most critical piece in the coaching process, and often overlooked. Don't skip this, as it provides the reinforcement needed for making actual behavioral change. Get it scheduled and you'll get it done.

Create clear goals.

In several of her meetings with Ben and Darryl, Stephanie asked what they planned to do differently once they left her office. Essentially, she helped her emerging leaders create tangible goals. These were often short-term and focused, but they provided clear, achievable targets.

Be transparent.

Stephanie broke the norm by ensuring goals were published and department metrics were posted on her office window. Her transparency created an open environment of communication and a focus on ownership, both of which helped improve communication within her team and across departments. It also allowed her to focus on solving problems with her people instead of merely sharing information.

Communicate through monthly town hall meetings.

Stephanie was able to extend her coaching to the larger organization through her monthly town hall meetings. To make these effective, she engaged her people by:

- Removing physical barriers typically found in conference rooms and cafeterias.

- Asking team members to submit questions prior to the meeting. This elevated the level of participation and ownership people had in the meetings.

- Communicating what she knew and did not know. Most of the pain people experience from change has more to do with the stories they tell themselves than with the change itself. Communicating what you know and don't know can alleviate that pain.

- Inviting team members to give short presentations on various personal and professional topics. Giving center stage to people who were not in supervisory positions was critical to making the town halls work.

- Following up meetings with action items and asking for additional input to ensure that she captured what she heard. At the start of the next town hall, Stephanie would review the status of the action items from the previous month's meeting to demonstrate her commitment to her people.

While this book has focused primarily on the emerging leader, its principles are applicable to leaders at all levels. Most important, when leaders take the time to put their people first, they ignite the potential of each individual, and of the organization as a whole.

A Climbing and Mountaineering Terms

5.9+—rating system that describes the level of difficulty of a rock-climbing route goes from 5.0–5.15. A climb in the 5.9+ range would be considered an intermediate level of difficulty.

Anchor—system of one or more pieces of gear built to secure a climber to rock or snow as he or she belays another climber

Belay—process limiting the potential fall distance of a climber by passing the rope through a friction-enhancing belay device

Couloir—formation on the side of a mountain resembling a narrow chute or steep gulley typically filled with ice and/or snow

Crampons—metal spikes used by mountaineers and ice climbers that attach to the bottom of climbing boots and provide purchase into snow and ice to help keep an alpinist secure

Crevasse—large and often deep opening in a glacier, created by the movement of parts of the ice and the topography

Haul system—system created by a climber using pulleys, ropes, and other gear to extract a climber who has fallen into a crevasse

Heel hook—rock-climbing technique whereby a climber typically places a foot near head level and uses the heel in a pulling fashion to complete a move

Ice screw—long, tubular screw, about 18–23 cm, used to protect an ice climber

Lead (lead climber)—form of climbing in which the first climber leads a pitch, places protection, and climbs above it, then repeats the process until the pitch is complete. The lead climber typically belays a second climber up to his or her anchor.

Overhang—section of rock that is angled beyond ninety degrees and often looms overhead

Picket—long, narrow aluminum device, typically 2–3 feet in length, that mountaineers place in snow to build anchors

Pitch—usually about the length of a rope (50–60 meters). A climb may be one or more pitches.

Piton—flat, metal blade of steel hammered into rock to provide protection for a climber

Traverse—climbing in a horizontal direction across or along a rock, snow, or ice face

About the Author

Sal Silvester is founder and president of **5.12 Solutions** (five-twelve), an organizational development company based in Boulder, Colorado. Senior leaders call on Sal and his team of talented facilitators to help them ignite the potential of their people, resulting in a highly engaged workforce, reduced turnover, and organizational ability to capitalize on business opportunities. Sal's unique perspective on team and leadership development comes from twenty years of experience as an Army officer and an executive at Accenture, and in hundreds of client engagements through the company he founded, **5.12 Solutions**.

A graduate of the U.S. Army Ranger and Airborne schools, Sal is passionate about rock climbing, ice climbing, and mountaineering, and has traveled the United States and South America in pursuit of the ultimate climbing adventure. He has competed in six marathons and is an Ironman Triathlon finisher.

Sal's *People-First* electronic newsletter and Sal's Blog (**http://www.512solutions.com/Blog**) both focus on helping ignite the potential of leaders and generating team member commitment.

To learn more about Sal and 5.12 Solutions, visit
http://www.512solutions.com.

About 5.12 Solutions

5.12 Solutions helps organizations ignite the potential of their people, enabling them to accelerate business results and become employers of choice. Learn more at http://www.512solutions.com.

People-First Leadership™ Development Program: Are your emerging leaders prepared for roles that will directly impact business results? This nine-month program is designed for people who are considered high potential and are potentially future senior leaders within your organization, and we know it will ignite their performance.

The Senior Leadership Team Development Program™: Is your management team struggling to achieve its highest level of effectiveness, and as a result missing out on opportunities? This 6–9 month program is designed for management teams that want to make a major shift in how they work together.

The Team Acceleration Program™: Are your teams struggling with communication breakdowns and unnecessary conflict, and as a result wasting precious time and energy? This 6–12 month program is designed for new and existing teams that want to make a significant shift in how they communicate and collaborate, enabling them to achieve the results they were meant to achieve.

Other Happy About® Books

Purchase these books at Happy About http://happyabout.com or at other online and physical bookstores.

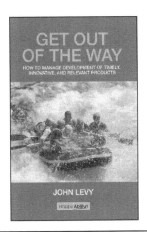

Get Out of the Way

This book is a must have for all managers of engineering, software-development, IT, and other high-tech development organizations, as well as the executives who do business with them.

Paperback $19.95
eBook $14.95

#MOJO tweet

#MOJOtweet by *New York Times* best-selling author Marshall Goldsmith reveals how we can create Mojo in our lives, maintain it, and recapture it when we need it.

Paperback $19.95
eBook $14.95

Scrappy General Management

This book will provide you with the 7 common-sense and repeatable steps that will guide you through running a business that everyone will be proud to be associated with.

Paperback $19.95
eBook $14.95

The 24-Hour Turnaround

The authors, Jeffrey S. Davis and Mark Cohen, are uniquely qualified to write this book—a compilation of case studies highlighting entrepreneurial styles, innovations, and triumphs.

Paperback $19.95
eBook $14.95